JOURNEY MAN

JOURNEY MAN

Celebrating an Unlucky, Unpredictable, and Undeniably Successful NBA Career

by

TOM VAN ARSDALE

with

TYLER DASWICK

BANQUO PRESS

JOURNEY MAN

ISBN 978-163684271-4 (paperback)
ISBN 978-163684270-7 (eBook)
ISBN 978-163684272-1 (hback)

10 9 8 7 6 5 4 3 2 1

Cover design by Milan Jovanovic, Chameleon Studio
Interior Design by Diana Vara

Banquo Press
Scottsdale, AZ

This book is dedicated to my wife, Kathy,
my children, Kerrie (Scott), Chris (Caroline), Amy (Justin),
and my grandchildren, Charlie, Tommy, Oscar, and Minna.
I thank them for their love and support.

INTRODUCTION

I'd like to introduce myself. My name is Tom Van Arsdale, also known as "not Dick," who is my identical twin brother. It's easy to confuse Dick and me. We both played basketball at Emmerich Manual High School, Indiana University and in the NBA for 12 seasons.

It doesn't bother me when I'm called by my brother's name. That's part of being an identical twin. When we were drafted into the NBA, it was the first time we were separated—Dick went to the Knicks 10th overall in 1965 and I went 11th overall to the Detroit Pistons—but while our careers mirrored one another statistically, our paths through the sport diverged.

While my brother's career saw him become the Original Sun, compete in a number of playoff games and even play for the Suns in the 1976 Finals against the Boston Celtics, I never had such a thrill in the NBA. I played 929 games, scored 14,232 points, averaged 15.3 points per game, and made three All Star teams, but I still hold the record—43 years running now—of having scored the most points in NBA history without competing in a playoff game. How could that be possible? I certainly was not a superstar, but I was considered a star player and was somewhat recognizable among the public. I played with all-time greats like Dave DeBusschere, Jerry Lucas, Connie Hawkins, and even my personal hero, the legendary Oscar Robertson. And yet, the best record one of my teams ever earned was 41-41. Maybe that comes from facing Bill Russell and Wilt Chamberlain 16 times per year. Maybe that comes from being traded five times. Maybe that's just rotten luck. I don't know.

Some people might assume my place in NBA history would lead this book to be a "woe is me" sob story about the challenges of my career, but I don't want to be like that. The truth is, I cherish my NBA career. I loved my time in the league, and the strong relationships I have with my basketball contemporaries still mean a great deal to me. I shared the court with awe-inspiring teammates, astonishing opponents, larger-than-life coaches, and yeah, my twin brother, too. Professional basketball gave me a sense of kinship and brotherhood with other NBA veterans that persists to this day. Even though my career had its share of bad luck, I don't think that makes me an unlucky person. I loved every minute of playing in the NBA. It was a dream come true.

Welcome to *Journey Man*, a celebration of my exciting, volatile, heartbreaking, strange, beloved, wouldn't-trade-it-for-anything career in basketball. This is the NBA as I saw it, my ongoing testimony to the daily triumphs, defeats, elations, and disappointments of being a professional basketball player. Across 12 years, I experienced enough excitement to fill a book. How could you call that anything but a success?

Thanks for coming along,

T.V.

Chapter One

Grandpa Bert stepped off the ladder and gestured for Dick and me to admire his handiwork. "How about that, boys?"

I looked up. *Woah. That sure is high.* My twin brother stood next to me and looked up, too. Grandpa Bert had nailed the backboard and basket snug against the tree. I thought it looked beautiful. I was five years old. I had never thought anything looked beautiful before. "Thanks, Grandpa!" Dick and I said.

Grandpa Bert smiled. "Every boy needs a basketball hoop," he said, and from around his back he brought forth a brand-new basketball—smooth, leathery, with so much bounce it felt it might burst. Dick and I clung to it as if it would escape. "What are you waiting for?" Grandpa Bert asked. "Let's see some shots."

And Dick and I ran onto the court.

I fell in love with basketball before I knew it as a competition. My earliest sports memories aren't associated with winning and losing at all. I just loved to play. When I remember my childhood days playing pickup games in Indiana, I think more about the dusty courts, homemade baskets, and larger-than-life characters than the hard-fought victories or tough losses. Basketball used to be simple that way.

In Greenwood, Indiana—population 2,500 in those days—your first basketball hoop was a rite of passage. Our town was only 44 miles north of Bloomington, home of Indiana University and the Hoosier teams that everyone, and I mean *everyone*, loved to death. Indiana's men's basketball coach, Branch McCracken, had become a statewide hero in 1940 for leading the Hoosiers to their first NCAA championship, but as I was growing up in the early '50s, he evolved from a local idol into a titanic figurehead before some of the greatest Indiana teams ever assembled. His players—Don Schlundt, Bobby Leonard, Dick Farley—became legends in their own right, and my brother and I could recite the statistics for everyone up and down the roster. We tracked each guy's totals, game by game, as the season progressed, visiting our neighbor's house in Greenwood to watch the games on television. In our town it was the luckiest thing in the world to know somebody with a TV, so our neighbor's house became the gathering place for anyone interested in the Hoosiers' quest for another championship. Of course, in Greenwood, "anyone interested" really meant everyone.

Dick and I wanted to be just like our college heroes, so when Grandpa Bert was measuring our backyard hoop, we urged him to put it up to 10 feet high. He did the best he could, which was about the best anybody could do back then. Maybe our hoop was 10'1" (I always felt the rim was oddly just a bit out of reach), but it didn't make much difference when Dick and I were beginning to play. We could barely muscle the ball to the basket. I still remember the day Dick found the strength and form to shoot with one hand. I was heaving the ball at the rim like a volleyball setter, and I turned and saw him crooking his elbow and flicking his wrist like it was the most natural thing in the world. I was in awe. I remembering thinking: *When the heck will I ever be strong enough to shoot like Dick?* I had to practice some more.

Our hoop debuted above a grass court, but the more Dick and I played, the more we wore down the grass until we had to just call it a dirt court. That worked in our favor. Near

4

the basket, where Dick and I drove for layups and fought for rebounds, the ground was hard and well-weathered, but farther from the hoop, patches of grass sprung up like pockmarks (this was before the introduction of the three-point line, so we didn't exactly space the floor like the pros do today). And where the grass really started to grow again—well, that was the sideline. We literally stamped our court into existence.

The more Dick and I played on that court, the more we learned all of its quirks. There was a series of ridges on the right wing that threw off your dribble if you weren't careful, and there was a hole at center court that meant you had to flare out on a fast break, giving the defender a little extra step on the recovery. We learned to leverage all the idiosyncrasies to our advantage, and that ended up inadvertently preparing me for some of the stadiums in the pros. The Boston Garden, for example, was infamous for having soft floorboards and soft rims. You had to watch where you dribbled because sometimes you'd bounce the ball in the wrong place, and it wouldn't come back the way you'd expect. I was able to pick up those nuances easily in the pros, and I bet it had a lot to do with playing on my backyard court as a kid.

As my brother and I grew up, our dirt court grew with us. Our dad measured out another basket so we could play full court (the grass on that half of the yard wore out in a hurry, too), and he put up a light so we could play after the sun went down. Sometimes when Dick and I were shooting at night, Mom and Dad would bring out folding chairs to the sidelines and watch. They never cheered for one of us over the other. Everything was fair between Dick and me, from our time on the basketball court to the amount of orange juice we were served with breakfast.

My brother and I were an even match on the court, too, though that didn't mean we took it easy on one another. We absolutely didn't. When we began playing in college and the NBA, we became known for our aggressive style, and there are seeds of that in our early 1-on-1 games. Sometimes we'd piss one another off so much we'd start full-on fighting (the only rule: body shots only, nothing to the face), only laying off after we had matured a little in high school.

A common afternoon of games between Dick and me went like this: We'd agree to play best two out of three, but after one of us took the series, the other would be so pissed he'd challenge to best three out of five, or best four out of seven. And we'd keep going back and forth until we had won an even number of games. Plenty of times it would be late in the day, the sun would be going down on our couple of acres in Greenwood, and mom would call us inside to dinner, but if Dick had me 2 games to 1, I'd wave Mom off like she was a coach asking me to sub out and go at my brother so hard there was just no way he was going to beat me. After I won, we'd have 2 games apiece, so we'd go inside and wash up for dinner. We were both happy that way.

***

My brother and I turned 10 years old a few weeks before the 1953 NCAA tournament, and wouldn't you know it, Indiana University was the No. 1 overall seed that year. That Hoosiers team was one of the best I'd ever seen. A 23-3 overall record, a 16-game winning streak in the Big Ten, and five players who'd go on to the NBA the nest season: Bobby Leonard, Dick Farley, and Don Schlundt. My brother and I knew the team inside and out. Schlundt was the star—he led the Hoosiers with a gaudy 25 points per game—but Bobby Leonard, the starting guard, would go on to become a true icon in Indiana. After his time in Bloomington, Leonard played seven seasons in the NBA before coming back to Indiana to coach the Pacers and do some play-by-play commentary for the pros. His lifestyle became infamous—he was a well-known gambler, and drinker, —but it hardly mattered to anyone in our home state. If you found basketball success in Indiana, your reputation was hard to spoil.

The same year that 1953 team torched a path to the tournament, our family bought our own television set. That was a big deal. Dick and I could sit and watch Indiana basketball in our living room. It felt like the team didn't just belong to Greenwood anymore; they were showing up in our house, playing just for us. That NCAA tournament run cast a kind of magic spell over Dick and me. By the time the Hoosiers beat the defending champion Kansas Jayhawks in the final behind Don Schlundt's 30 points and Charley Kraak's 17 points and 13 rebounds, there was no question in our minds: We were going to play basketball for Indiana University someday.

***

There was a long way to go before Dick and I could take the floor for the Hoosiers, so we started playing organized basketball in fifth grade. Our coach, Floyd Coverstone, was the nicest, most patient, most encouraging man a couple kids could ask to teach them the sport. In fact, he was maybe a little too instructive. After our very first practice, he called the team to take a knee around him, reached into his back pocket, and pulled out a bright white jock strap. Then he explained to a group of wide-eyed 10- and 11-year-olds how to put on said jock strap, complete with a demonstration right over his khaki pants. None of us knew what to think—we didn't even know what a jock strap was—but I suppose someone had to do it. That was Coach Coverstone. He didn't want us to look like fools, even if it meant looking like a fool himself.

Basketball was all about having fun back then. We didn't even think about competition. The first game I ever played was against a little town called Nineveh in Johnson County. It was such a small community that today I'm not sure it's even recognized as a city by the state of Indiana, but they had a little school out there with maybe 50 kids in it, and they somehow found a basketball team among those 50 kids, so our team hopped on a school bus and went out to the Ninevah to play the...well, I guess the Ninevites.

I can't help but evoke the Old Testament: We absolutely smote the Ninevites. But riding the bus back to Greenwood, I don't think we really comprehended the victory. We were too young to be competitive. I just thought about how much fun I had and how good it felt to score. When Dick and I arrived back at school and saw Mom and Dad, we ran up to them, gushing. "Hey! We won, and I had 11 points! And Dick had seven!" I said. Dick yammered on next to me, and we had the basketball bug. Coach Coverstone came over and told our parents, "Your boys played pretty well tonight." And it felt great to have a coach say that. I didn't think about winning or losing, but I did think about playing well again. I knew I wanted to play more games, and hopefully do okay in those games, too.

***

There are two stages of realizing you're good at something: The first is when you realize you're good at something, and the second is when you see someone who's so much better than you at the thing you're good at that you go right back down to feeling like you aren't that good again. That's exactly what happened to me when I first laid eyes on my basketball hero Oscar Robertson, during his debut game for Crispus Attucks High School in 1954.

It was the beginning of one of the most decorated and impressive runs in the history of Indiana basketball. Oscar's first season at Attucks, the team advanced all the way to the state semi-finals before losing to the eventual champion, Milan (that was the famous *Hoosiers* team). When Oscar was a junior, Attucks went 31-1 and won the state title, the first time an all-black school had ever done that in the United States. Attucks repeated as champions the next year, never losing a game, and Oscar was named Mr. Indiana Basketball, our state's crowning individual honor for a high school player.

I had never seen anyone play like Oscar. No one in Indiana had ever seen anyone like Oscar. He was smoother than a five-dollar milkshake, sturdier than a Rocky mountain, smarter than a Russian chess player, and faster than an Indiana copperhead snake. Everything he did on the court felt like the purest distillation of that particular skill. His passes skipped like stones on a still lake. His shot splashed like singular rain drops. On defense, he was a towering wave. Oscar was tall in the huddle and poised before the crowd—especially the hostile, racist crowds—and all around he was a complete basketball perfectionist. I said he was my hero. Correction: He's my hero to this day.

I first met Oscar face-to-face away from basketball. We were at the same track meet in Bloomington, Indiana, when I was about 12 years old. I was walking to my seat when I spotted him standing by the concession stand, holding one of those foot-long hot dogs, a coney, smothered in mustard and relish. I knew it was him. He was wearing his letterman jacket from Crispus Attucks, loaded with patches and pins. My pre-teen brain was struck dumb. This was the moment. This was the perfect time to go up to Oscar Robertson and ask for his autograph.

I took a deep breath, summoned all my courage, and approached him. I held my arms stiff at my sides like a robot and I had my head tilted a little bit down to the ground, like a missile. I was on a mission. "H-h-h-hey Oscar?" I asked.

Oscar turned and looked at me, his eyebrows up. He could tell I was nervous right away. "Hey there," he said. His mouth was full of hot dog and he swallowed with a gulp. He covered his mouth with a hand. "Sorry," he said. "How are you?"

"I was wondering if I could have your autograph," I said. I was already tall by then, but I felt like a pin. "Please," I added. I glanced up into his eyes. Oscar looked a little surprised, but his expression was kind, even breezy.

Oscar smiled. Wow, he had a superhero smile. "Of course I will. Here," he said, and without the slightest hesitation, he shoved his loaded foot-long hot dog right in the front pocket of his letterman jacket. It poked a good four or five inches out of the top like a baguette in a shopping bag. Oscar didn't pay it any mind. He reached for my pen and paper and signed his name, nice and clear. He handed me the signature. "Take care!"

I stared at the paper. "Th-th-th-thanks," I said.

Oscar retrieved his hot dog from his pocket and waved it at my thank-you, as if deflecting it. "Any time!"

I walked to my seat clutching the signature like it was a treasure map. I still have it now, 64 years later. Looking at it, it's a wonder there aren't any condiment stains on it.

***

Sometimes I think growing up in Indiana and witnessing so much incredible basketball as a kid—Oscar, Crispus Attucks, Milan, the 1953 Hoosiers—was both a lucky and unlucky experience. It was a golden age for basketball, a near-unconceivable stretch of seminal players, coaches, and teams, but as I prepared to play in high school myself, I began to feel a lot of pressure to find a place among all those heroes. I still loved to scrap with Dick in our backyard and practice my shooting and score, but the competition side of basketball became weightier and more prominent as I grew older. I'd lie awake at night thinking about what it might be like to compete for a state championship, and I'd lose sleep worrying I'd never make it to that kind of stage. Indiana was a one-class state. Over 600 teams competed in the same field for one single title. Would I ever be good enough, or lucky enough, to break out of that field and have a shot at a championship? I'd never be like Oscar. I had only learned how to put on a jock strap just a few years ago, and you know, why was it so hard to reach the rim in the backyard?

Basketball wasn't so simple anymore. The line between innocent sport and intense competition were starting to blur, and I struggled to parse the demands of winning and losing with my instinctive, natural love for the game. This tension would appear and reappear, time and again, over the course of my career. I didn't realize something I cherished as much as basketball could scare me so much, could maybe even hurt me. If basketball rejected me, I wasn't sure what I would do. It was what I loved most. What if after all these dreams, the sport just let me down?

Chapter Two

We hit the only stoplight in Greenwood, and we hit it on red. Inside the car, everybody was quiet. Dick and I were in the back seat and our parents were up front. It was just after one of our seventh-grade basketball games, an absolute blowout in which St. Mark's Middle School beat us 48-12. Neither Dick nor I had scored even a single point. Basketball had started to become more serious, and that day, it felt especially serious.

I crossed my arms and leaned my head against the window and stared out at the road. If there had been a postgame press conference, someone in the media might have asked me, "What happened out there, Tom?" But I had no idea, and Dick didn't have one, either. We were just plain whipped. St. Mark's had a kid on their team who must've matured early, because he looked like a monster—all arms and hair—and he used his outlier size and strength to dominate us. I don't remember his name, because honestly, he didn't go on to have any kind of notable career in Indiana basketball. That's still strange to me, that some random somebody out there can sprout into a prepubescent monster at 13 years old and munch on middle schoolers for a couple years before everyone catches up to them on the growth chart and they're washed out by high school. It reminds me that being good at sports for a long time takes some lucky timing. I don't know what happened to that St. Mark's kid, but he certainly mattered, because he contributed to one of the most vivid memories of my childhood.

I was watching the wind rustle the cornfield on the other side of the glass, feeling sorry for myself, when my father—Raymond—broke the silence.

"Hilda," he said to my mom, "I just can't take it anymore."

Dick looked forward. I picked up my head off the window.

My dad sighed out through his nose. His nostrils expanded and I saw his pores stretch. "I just can't take riding with these boys anymore," he said. "They were awful today." Dick and I glanced at one another. Dad continued. "You know what? If they're going to play like that, I'm not riding home with them." And he opened his door, stepped out of the car, shut the door behind him, and started walking toward home. It was a mile to our house.

Dick and I were frozen in the back. Mom didn't speak. The silence in the car gathered over us like a collection of storm clouds. If someone said something, it would have broken open. But we all were quiet. When the light turned green, my mom just let off the brake and moved through the intersection, passing my father on the right. He didn't even look at us. My brother and I peered at him through the window and Mom bent to check if he was okay, but nobody called out to him. Mom didn't slow down or try to argue. She just kept driving. We reached our house about 10 minutes before Dad, but once he came home, nobody mentioned what had happened. Dad didn't come in to talk to Dick and me, Mom didn't either, and we all just let the incident wither away. It's sort of funny: When I tell that story, I never say Dick and I were surprised at my dad's behavior. We weren't. That was just Dad.

My father was a teacher at Indianapolis' Emmerich Manual High School, where Dick and I eventually went to school. He coached track there—he had been a star in the broad jump when he was young—in addition to football and basketball. Dad was a hard-working and high-standards man, and he applied his critical eye to everything from our basketball careers to his students' math exams to the organic strawberries he grew on our property. He was a multi-faceted self-starter and proud of it, but he utilized his wide range of skills all across the Greenwood community. He sang hymns with the Sunday choir at Greenwood Presbyterian—I'd always be nervous for him when he had a solo—and people would come from all over Johnson County to buy his strawberries. We sold out every picking of those strawberries, and during the peak of the growing season each summer, Dick and I would go out in the field every other day to help gather the fruit with the rest of Dad's picking team. We filled 500 quarts of strawberries each time.

But my father's rigor had some negative manifestations, especially with regards to athletics. Throughout my amateur career, he issued some criticisms that really affected the way I saw my ability and potential. What still stands out to me about that car ride home isn't that he was disappointed in the lack of effort between Dick and myself, but that he was unhappy with our performance, period. All my best mentors have emphasized that what makes a valuable teammate or performance is hustle, intention, and preparation. Your effort was more important than winning or losing. Dad, however, was results oriented. He cared first and foremost if Dick and I won. So even if we had good statistics in a defeat, or were outmatched by a talented opponent, it wouldn't sit well with Dad, and he'd express his disappointment. I know he came from a place of love and a desire for us to be successful, but it was challenging as a young man to internalize those responses alongside what my coaches were saying about doing your best and giving your maximum effort. I didn't understand how a coach could be proud of me after a loss, but my dad could be so disappointed over the same thing. It shook my confidence. *How did I know I was any good?*

Obviously, that incident with my dad is something I've never forgotten, but to this day, I don't hate him for it. My dad had a negative attitude—he was not a smiler—but he was a good man. I love him, still.

***

Mom, meanwhile, was the opposite from Dad. I have a go-to phrase to describe my mom: She could walk through a field of shit and say it smells like clover. That was instrumental in our family; Mom was somebody to lean on. She grew up a farmer's daughter in Indiana—milking cows, curing hams, driving farm equipment at 10 years old—so she had a foundation of dedication and industriousness that formed her into a natural pillar of strength. Our family saw its share of challenges as Dick and I grew up and left home, but Mom was always our anchor. She was a fixture not just in our home—for me and Dick and Dad late in his life—but for anyone else in Greenwood who needed her (including, believe it or not, future Indiana basketball coach Bobby Knight—but that's a story for later). We were lucky.

Mom and Dad's diametric dispositions established a pair of warring factions in my head when I was a young. On one side, I had my self-doubt and negativity, stoked by the intense standards of my dad and the heavy expectations I put over myself. I wanted to be a great basketball player, but that meant I couldn't see it as merely a backyard pastime or after-school hobby anymore. It was something I was pursuing and developing. I had to work on it. The work didn't scare me—I still don't really know how to give less than 100 percent—but I was intimidated by all of the worst-case scenarios I conjured in my mind. *What if I didn't win enough in high school? What if I couldn't play at Indiana? What if I fell short of reaching the pros?* When circumstances envelop me, my doubts sound louder than just about anything else, and no amount of points in the box score or tallies in the win column can silence them. It feels like I have to pull myself out, and I usually can't on my own. That's why I needed voices like Mom's.

Because when I received encouragement from Mom and the various saints and shepherds I met throughout my career, it coalesced into an opposing force that moved against my self-degradation. Positive reinforcement gave me the vision to see that I actually was pretty good, that I could contribute and make an impact. It empowered me to grit my teeth and keep going, and so over time, I honed a toughness against my own insecurities.

That's one of the paradoxes of my career. Even though I so often stepped onto the court with questions in my head about whether I deserved to be there or whether I was good enough, I had the resilience to keep stepping on the court and face those questions. I don't think that kind of contradiction is natural in a person, so when I reflect on that from my current vantage point,

17

I really believe it's evidence of grace in my life, God surrounding me and instilling me with what I needed to stay the course. I faced disappointments and frustrations in basketball that—believe it or not—far exceeded the 48-12 loss against St. Mark's—but I always caught vision for what was on the other side of those disappointments. I guess I have a little Mom in me, too.

I think lifelong athletes—particularly those who make it to the pros—have an easier time than you would think shaking off disappointments. In basketball, and most other sports, fans tend to focus on the way players handle high-stakes occasions like playoff games and championship series. That, to many, is the truest measure of grit and determination: if you can come up big in the clutch. But every NBA player experiences countless gut-check moments: losing streaks during the regular season, overtime defeats, nights when a great individual performance was swept up in a loss. Those things stack up on the shoulders of any athlete. Losing is part of the job, but most guys grow accustomed to letting setbacks fade in their short-term memory. We learn to leave it behind and focus on the next game—just like anyone at an office can put a tough day at work behind them and go back tomorrow. Losing isn't going to kill you. There's usually another chance to be successful at something, in life and in sports.

Now, I recognize this is coming from someone who never made the playoffs. I'm sure there's a different tone to losing a playoff series, because that is the true end of something. One player who has taught me a lot about that is former Los Angeles Lakers guard Jerry West. Jerry is one of the greatest players to ever grace the NBA. He made the All-Star team all 14 years of his career, averaged 27 points per game over his career, and earned 10 first-team All-Pro selections. His Lakers won the NBA championship in 1971, too. By all accounts, he's one of the league's most celebrated and decorated stars.

But Jerry also lost the NBA Finals eight times, more than any other player in history. His playoff performances were always spectacular—during the 1965 playoffs, when he was just 26 years old, he averaged 40.6 points per game—but thanks to a combination of bad luck and poor matchups against Bill Russell's Boston Celtics, winning a championship proved a white whale for Jerry. The continuous losing devastated him, so much that when he finally won the title, it didn't seem to grant him much peace. We've talked about his career a lot, and I think he remembers it with a lot of regret, even though the vast majority of his peers would trade legacies with him in a second. It's a mystery to me. Elgin Baylor lost seven Finals and doesn't share Jerry's attitude. Oscar, too, had plenty of struggles during his time in the pros, but he's not depressed over it. If Jerry feels like he could've done more to further his success in the NBA, I'm not sure what he sees. He was incredible. At the same time, I know what it's like to struggle with depression. It's hard to have perspective under that shadow. I wish Jerry knew how much we admired him.

There are plenty of moments in my basketball career when it would have made a lot of sense to lose myself over an outcome whether it was in my control or completely beyond it, but I was always able to look up. That feels fortunate. With the career I had, I needed all the optimism and positivity I could find.

***

Oh, I almost forgot to mention this, but later during our seventh-grade season, Dick and I played St. Mark's and that monster kid again. The second time, we beat the absolute shit out of them: 55-29. What can I say? We were tough.

Chapter Three

Even Sparky the Bus Driver was quiet. Next to him in the frontmost seat, Coach Cummins sat holding his face in his hands.

It was a 25-minute drive back to Manual High School from Butler Fieldhouse after the state championship, but it felt like we were on the road for hours. Snow fell outside, and the wind rattled the bus as we moved down the icy Indianapolis streets. I sat next to Dick and stared at nothing. I wished I could vanish and reappear at home in Greenwood. When I thought about going back to school, I just felt worse.

The Manual booster club and spirit squad—in anticipation of us bringing home the trophy—had built a celebratory bonfire on our football field. They hadn't made a backup plan. But when we pulled into the parking lot, you could see the fire nonetheless, with the cheerleaders, students, and parents huddled around it. The marching band was half-arranged to one side, their instruments down and away. Most people had their faces down, their arms crossed against the cold.

Sparky parked the bus and the team filed off, but I stayed in my seat and looked out the window. I didn't see much. I was too far in my own head, thinking about the final moments of the game, the missed opportunities, the tears, the kids from Kokomo High leaping in circles with their arms in the air. I know it's a cliché, but it felt like a robbery. That's what most disappointment feels like, as if something's been stolen from you. You don't see what's there; you just see what's not. Just the loss.

***

Modern high school leagues use class systems to separate powerhouse programs from small-time institutions, but Indiana's state basketball championship threw every school into the same postseason tournament—over 600 teams. It was a cruel, alluring, multi-week event that ran the winners through an epic gauntlet of sectional, regional, and semifinal brackets before the final bracket—the final four—decided the title. It was March Madness to the extreme, a showcase for scrappy middle-of-nowhere schools, bottom-seeded cinderellas, and perennial dominators. Throughout the history of the tournament, individual players had carved out legends for themselves with impressive, history-making runs. Some of those kids went on to become NBA stars, like Terry Dischinger taking tiny Garfield High past the sectionals in 1955, or Oscar Robertson winning back-to-back state titles for Crispus Attucks in '55 and '56. There are famous Indiana teams, too. Future pros Greg Oden and Mike Conley gave Lawrence North High School three straight titles in the early 2000s (after Indiana introduced a class system), and who could forget the Milan team that inspired *Hoosiers*?

Winning state was the holy grail of amateur basketball in Indiana. For some, it was a life-defining achievement—anyone who wins wears it as part of their identity—and I have peers who reminisce to this day about their championships. These are guys who never made the pros, or even played in college, but they have a title, and that makes them somebody. I know plenty of guys who came up short, too, who still can't shake the loss. I understand that kind of defeat. You don't know what you're missing, and that's the worst part—not knowing.

My imagination used to run wild with dreams of a championship victory at Butler Fieldhouse, long before I had the opportunity to play in the tournament. In grade school and middle school, I actually lay awake at night imagining the crowd, the lights, the trophy, the cheers and applause. Sometimes my daydreams would become fraught with anxiety and I'd lose sleep over those dreams. *What if I never even made it past regionals? What if I never had the chance to see Butler? What if I did make it, but then I lost? Would it be worth it?* I'd toss and turn in my basketball wilderness while Butler Fieldhouse glittered in the distance: my pillar of fire, my mecca, the promised land.

***

In 1957, Dick and I enrolled at Emmerich Manual High School amid a steady rise to prominence in the local sports community. We had improved so much since our early days on the basketball court that our decision to attend Manual—about 10 miles from our house, on the south side of Indianapolis— had stirred up some controversy in Greenwood. Our town had apparently been anticipating the day the Van Arsdale twins would arrive at Greenwood High and lift the local team to statewide recognition, but honestly, Dick and I had always considered Manual a better choice. It was where our father taught and coached and where our mother had a clerical job, but beyond that, playing in Indianapolis pitted us against tougher competition within a more talented section of schools. Dick and I endured a few sore letters to the paper and some mild chatter around town, but there was no question we made the right decision.

That type of criticism was par for the course in Indiana. Just as Texans flock to the football field and Minnesotans commune around the hockey rink, so do Indianans covet the basketball court. It really is like a religion. Families, communities, entire towns build their identities around the local team. As the wins come in, so the town booms. As the losses compound, so does the malaise.

There were no professional sports teams in Indiana in those days except a AAA baseball team called the Indianapolis Indians, so high school basketball was all people had to pull them away from working on the farm and driving through the countryside and listening to whatever else was on the radio. Only a few families had TVs, so kids went outside, found a court, and played basketball. Baskets hung on barns and silos, the more fortunate families hosted their neighborhoods around their TVs to watch the state tournament, and every local business prided itself as the preferred drive-in, deli, barbershop, or diner of the local high school athletic programs.

Our Manual teams held territory over the south side of Indianapolis. Shapiro's Deli on Meridian Street would wave us inside after practice for corned beef sandwiches the size of bricks and chips piled up to your eyeballs (often on the house). The Tee Pee Drive-In on Madison waved in gangs of us teenage boys on weekend nights for burgers and hot dogs, and the server girls would roll out to our cars and take our orders beneath the real life-sized teepee on the roof. The local newspapers wrote up our games so often that Dick and I would be surprised when we *didn't* make the sports pages, and when we walked around campus and around town, we'd be recognized quite a bit. Being a twin probably helped with that.

Basketball players in Indiana are celebrities. These days, I find being called out in public to be a little embarrassing—especially when I'm with my family—but as a kid doing nothing but playing the sport I loved, there was no better life.

For all the small-town fame we enjoyed, the bigger stage at Manual brought bigger demands for my brother and me. As a city, Indianapolis expected success—they had a history of great teams and players—so it wasn't a Greenwood-esque "just happy to be here" situation. Dick and I went to Manual because of the more intense competition, but that raised the pressure on us as much as it honed our physical toughness. Maybe that risk would turn off some kids, but Dick and I always sought out the steepest hill to climb. We wanted to play in difficult environments. We figured that's how you improved.

I think most professional athletes are supreme self-motivators. To reach the pros, you have to rely a great deal on your own work ethic, because the quality of play the pros ask for can't really be demanded by anyone except yourself. You have to achieve a level of mastery or expertise in the NBA, while most "regular" jobs only require competency. Anyone can teach somebody to be competent, but it takes a true self-motivated individual to find that special brand of excellence that puts you in a higher class.

Also, as a current 77-year-old, I have to tell you: As hard as Dick and I worked, we both were terrific athletes. No one dunked very often in those days, but I could slam one down

25

when I wanted. I had a 37-inch vertical leap (in hard-rubber Converse All-Stars, no less—these details matter), a quick first step, strong hands, and sure coordination. I was a track star as well in high school, and one baseball season I tossed a no-hitter and ranked near the top of our division in home runs. My twin and I had a work ethic that urged us to out-hustle, out-labor, and out-practice just about everyone we knew. It's why we made the pros, and it's for sure why we went to Manual instead of Greenwood, but let's be clear: There was some God-given ability at work. Even if we had sat on our laurels and went to Greenwood High, Dick and I probably would have kicked the shit out of everyone anyway.

***

Now, at the risk of throwing my humility out the window completely, I want to say something else: It's a hell of a lot of fun to be one of the best players on a basketball team.

Our senior year at Manual, Dick and I were two of the top players in the state of Indiana. We dominated opponents. I was a double-digit scorer throughout high school, and my senior year I pushed the needle toward 20 points per game. Few things brought me greater pleasure than scoring. I was a decent shooter from outside, but I was at my best attacking the basket, and that aggression became one of my strongest assets in high school and beyond.

J.J. Redick is a current shooting guard for the New Orleans Pelicans. He's made a career out of being a three-point specialist, and he's pretty good—he has a lifetime three-point shooting percentage of 41 percent. I've heard J.J. describe on multiple occasions the intense thrill he feels when he sees his shot swish through the net—he says he feels that surge of pleasure every time it happens. That's exactly how scoring felt for me when I played, and when I scored a lot—man, those were good nights. Finding my groove on the court was a blast. Exhilarating. This reward system of sorts made it easy to fall in love with basketball, and it incentivized me to work hard and continue improving my game.

We didn't have the three-point line when I played, but even so, few things satisfied me as much as drilling a long-range jump shot. My favorite spot on the floor was the deep corner, where modern three-point specialists thrive due to the notch in the arc, but I was a more dangerous player close to the basket. Though my position was technically similar to the modern wing players, I scored much more around the basket than the small forwards in today's game. Fill in the blank with your preferred cliche of driving to the hoop—weaving through traffic, banging bodies, navigating the sea of arms—because whatever it looked like to charge into the lane and finish through contact, that was my sweet spot. Drawing a shooting foul on my way up to the rim and making the shot after contact was the best feeling. Those baskets didn't just indicate skill; they indicated imposition and power. You had to move into a space occupied by someone else and take control over it. There was a physical battle, and a mental battle, and an effort battle—a microcosm of competitive sports in a single drive, jump, and finish. At the peak of my abilities, I felt I had what it took to go up against anybody.

***

Aggression has to be in your nature to bruise a path to the NBA basket, so naturally, Indiana's culture encourages you to impose your will upon your opponents. If you really wanted to be tough, you went and played pickup in Indianapolis.

Dick and I entered the Indianapolis pickup scene in middle school, a transition both intimidating and awe-inspiring. I met many of my childhood heroes at pickup games, but it was a little strange, because at first, all my childhood heroes wanted to kick my ass. The games were straightforward "king of the court" rules, with the winners staying, so while everyone was playing, it was more important to win and maximize your playing time than make new friends. Guys were competitive, aggressive, and no-nonsense about the rules. I remember Dick and I would sit on the sidelines waiting our turn, watching guys like Bill Jones and Willie Gardner and Willie Meriweather do things we only dreamed of doing. We used to listen to their games on the radio. Now we might be playing *against* them?

One of our heroes actually doubled as our tour guide in the Indianapolis scene: a locally famous high school player named Carl Short. He went to Emmerich Manual, our future alma mater. Carl was well on his way to Indiana stardom at that time; he's in the Indiana Basketball Hall of Fame now. His senior season at Manual, he averaged 20 points and 13 rebounds before going to Newberry College in South Carolina and earning Little All-American honors. He was six years older than Dick and me—enough of a gap for us to listen to whatever he said.

While Dick and I were still just dipping our toes in the pickup games as two young middle schoolers, Carl took us from court to court to acclimate us to the competition. We rarely saw significant playing time against the older kids, but we did have enough clout as soon-to-be high schoolers for us to sit on the sidelines and watch and wait our turn. Usually, we watched Carl play, studying him to see how we should act once we were in his shoes.

Carl was, shall we say, a rugged player. He was physical and a little nasty and he always toed the line between bending the rules and committing fouls. As a high school star, this was to his tremendous advantage with referees, but in the self-litigated pickup games, the lack of regulation would sometimes tip him into the deep end. Carl wouldn't hesitate to foul you, but foul *him?* Oh boy. You were in for it.

One particular night game taught Dick and me a lot about Carl. We were on the sidelines watching him and a few other guys play 5-on-5, full court. The game was tightening up as time wound down, and players on both sides were starting to hand-check and throw their weight around a little more to stall the scoring. Carl was at center. During a late possession, he backed himself down into the post and called for the ball. His defender was right on his back like a "kick me" sign, sticking his chest out and lifting his arms wide to guard the pass.

It was tight defense, but Carl had moves. He faked a turn to his left, then spun back to his right, clearing his man with just the *tiniest* dig of his elbow. The defender stumbled, fooled by the fake and knocked off balance by the contact, and Carl rose for the wide-open layup. But the defender had other ideas. He whirled around and reached for Carl with both arms and took a swinging whack at the ball. *Smack.* Instead of the rubbery *thwop* of the ball springing free, there was just the sharp sting of skin-to-skin. The defender had effectively slapped Carl across his arm.

Carl yelled and threw up his arms and the ball went flying and he tumbled backward into the defender and both guys fell to the ground. The ball rolled out of bounds.

Carl was up first. He whirled on the defender. "Are you kidding me?"

The defender stood up, too, and put his hands on his knees and eyed Carl and shook his head. "You're playing like a lunatic, man."

"A lunatic?" Carl stepped forward. "Man, that's basketball. Get used to it." And Carl shoved the guy, hard, in the chest. In teenage-boy sign language, such a move only means one thing: *Let's fight.*

The defender scrambled back. I took a step onto the court to see past Dick for a better view. This next moment was crucial in every boy-to-boy confrontation. If the defender reciprocated, we had a scene on our hands. The defender caught himself, planted his feet, and set his jaw. He took two steps forward. *Uh oh.*

The defender shoved Carl right back. "Don't touch me."

It was Carl's turn to catch himself. His face went from intimidation mode to surprise to indignance in a single second. He came back forward. And he said something you rarely, rarely hear in a world where most playground shoving matches dissolve into nothing:

"Fight me, asshole."

Carl raised his fists. The defender raised his fists. Everyone ran toward them. Dick and I started running, too. There was the briefest of moments where it looked like both boys were teetering on the brink of violence, hesitating, unsure if they'd go through with it, and then Carl just hauled off and decked the guy.

Carl's fist hit the defender's forehead like a boxer hits a slab of beef. It was so square it sounded wet. *Ooh*, went everyone around the circle, and the defender crumpled. A gash opened on his brow and he covered it with his hands and blood seeped between his fingers. Everyone recoiled. Carl stood over the fallen defender, bouncing a little on his feet. Everyone's gaze moved from the defender to Carl. Carl felt the eyes on him, and he stopped bouncing. He dropped his hands. He looked around. The circle closed in on him. He searched for Dick and me. We made eye contact. "Guys, let's get the heck out of here," he said, and he jetted from the circle like a spooked raccoon.

The chase was on. Dick and I ran with Carl off the court and across the parking lot, leaping over car hoods and weaving through the rows of vehicles. Carl's car sat waiting at the far corner of the lot. Behind us, some of the other players were hollering and running after us, chucking water bottles and the basketball, even a shoe or two. We reached Carl's car. He unlocked the doors and Dick and I dove into the backseat while he ran around to the front and slid in and started the engine.

"Oh shit oh shit oh shit," Carl panted. He threw the car in reverse and hit the gas and the players in pursuit leapt out of the way and us three fugitives screamed out of the parking lot like the Hurryin' Hoosiers.

After a handful of sudden turns, two back-alley detours, and one blown stop sign, Carl deemed it safe to pull over and take stock of the situation. He stopped the car and turned around to look at us. He frowned. We were so scared we were practically sucking our thumbs. My heart was pounding. *Were we criminals?*

Carl's face became very serious. "Look, guys," he said. "Let me tell you something right now. If you ever get in a fight and you don't know how to box, make the first move. Slug the guy as soon and as hard as you can. And after that, you run like hell."

Dick and I nodded like our heads were on strings. *Okay, Carl. Absolutely, Carl. We hear you, Carl.*

Carl's eyes moved between the two of us. He seemed satisfied. He nodded. "Okay, good." He turned back around and sighed and adjusted the rearview so he could see us in the reflection. He raised his eyebrows. "So, I'll pick you guys up at the same time next week?"

And he did.

***

In the 1960s, your basketball community was defined by proximity, so Dick and I were fortunate to be adjacent to talented players, smart coaches, and passionate fans. Perhaps the best of them all: our coach at Manual, Indiana Basketball Hall of Famer Dick Cummins.

One of my lasting impressions of Coach Cummins, oddly, was how much my mother liked him. Cummins was a complete gentleman—handsome, stylish—and he had a confident handshake. He was very endearing, but if he wanted to have fun with you—and he often did with his players—he deployed a sly sense of humor. Cummins had lost half his right thumb in an ironworking accident, and when he wanted to make his athletes squirm, he'd reach for one of his solid handshakes, then dig his nub right into our palm. It was the worst feeling, stubby and unnatural, and I'd shiver whenever I touched it. Of course, that's exactly what Coach Cummins wanted, and it would just crack him up. Somehow you always ended up laughing with him. He had a great way with people.

Dick and I met Cummins after committing to Manual over Greenwood. That decision raised the ire of our neighbors and the local media, and every day it seemed like there was a new column in the paper, another disappointed look at the supermarket, and for me, another fresh doubt. *Would it have made more sense to stay close to home? Would it have just been easier that way?* Coach Cummins brought his outsize charisma right into that uncertainty. He knew exactly what it was like to be a scrutinized, influential figure in Indiana basketball, and moreover, he knew what it was like to rise to those circumstances and succeed in spite of them. With that knowledge, Cummins leveraged his privilege to legitimize people in his circle so they would benefit from his stamp of approval. That's exactly how he shepherded my brother and me through his program at Manual. We succeeded, in part, because he demonstrated to the public that he believed in us.

Cummins' first savvy move: Start Dick and me on the freshman team during our first year, instead of putting us right on the varsity. Being in the lower-stakes freshman games gave us room to adapt to the high-school environment and learn Cummins' system. Crucially, it also gave us an early opportunity to be leaders among our peers and experience team success— we went undefeated and won the city championship. After the freshman season, there were a few varsity games left to be played, so Coach Cummins called us up to play with the older kids. That was a big deal. I didn't think I'd make varsity until I was at least a junior. Manual went to the state tournament that year, and Cummins even gave Dick and me some minutes in the playoffs (our team eventually lost in the sectional round of the tournament).

I can't understate how important that affirmation and encouragement was for me—it was probably more significant than the athletic development I experienced over the same period. Cummins signaled things I desperately needed to hear: *You're supposed to be here. I want you on my team. You can help us succeed.* Sometimes our view of ourselves is so twisted it becomes essential for someone to step in and show us the truth of who we are. Those relationships change us on an emotional and spiritual level, and that was who Coach Cummins was to me. He confirmed my desires and my purpose.

***

But we can also be honest here: Cummins' faith in Dick and me was not ill-founded. After our freshman season, we started for his varsity team three straight seasons, growing into the focal points of his offense and the anchors of his defense. Our team went 17-6 our sophomore year (before losing in the sectionals again), and 24-3 our junior year (that season, we lost in the regional final after a questionable foul call—I still say the kid flopped).

Our senior season, however, Dick and I emerged as two of the finest players in the state of Indiana. Our team was dominant, 19-2 during the regular season and absolute terrors in the playoffs. As the fifth-ranked team in the state (out of 600, remember) we stormed through the sectionals and ripped through the regionals to reach the regional final for the second straight year. This time, our opponent was Crispus Attucks, the powerhouse program with heroic alumni like Hallie Bryant and Oscar Robertson. Attucks had the third-ranked team in the state in 1961. Their center, Bill Jones, was 6'8", and was a handful for us that year. We had played Attucks in a city tournament earlier in the season, and they had pounded us. We entered the final as pretty significant underdogs.

I remember Coach Cummins entering the locker room before the game and approaching the big chalkboard at the front of the room. "Alright, boys," he said. "Pay attention, because we're doing something to Attucks we've never done to anybody."

All us kids looked at each other with our eyebrows up to our hairlines. What was Coach thinking? You never tried a new scheme for the first time in the playoffs.

But if Cummins saw our skepticism, he just ignored it. He erased the board and grabbed a new piece of chalk and began scratching out a diagram of a fresh offensive set. "This is called the double post," he said. "Dick and Tom, that means you."

My brother smacked my leg. I felt my heart float up my throat a little.

"It's simple," Cummins said, pointing and tracing lines with his finger. "Dick and Tom post up on the blocks at either side of the basket. We want an entry pass to either of them from the outside, and that will force the Bill Jones kid"—here Cummins drew a bunch of lines between Dick and me that looked kind of like the parting of the Red Sea— "to clear the middle. That's when you guys on the outside cut through the lane"—big slashes through the Red Sea— "and Dick or Tom will find you for a layup. And if Jones doesn't commit to the block, or shades off, well"—Cummins looked at my brother and me— "you guys go to work on him."

Dick and I worked our way to 45 points that night. Attucks, as a team, had 44. Manual won going away. After the game, we shook hands with our opponents and headed to the locker room. I was walking alongside Cummins. "Good game, Tom," he said.

"Thanks, Coach."

"You're welcome. I knew I could trust you."

For the first time, I felt like I belonged in the tournament.

***

We had reached the last stop of the tournament: the final four at Butler Fieldhouse. I stepped onto the gleaming wooden floor and looked out at the 15,000 seats and thought: *What am I doing here?* It exceeded my every expectation. The lights were hot, the baskets gleamed, and the floor hadn't so much as a scuff. Even after the crowd arrived, the arena had a vastness to it that made it seem easy to lose myself, and easy for others to lose me, too. If I didn't rise to the occasion, all the glares and noise would wash me right out. I understand why they say athletes "shine" in big games, because if you don't stand out on stages like Butler Fieldhouse, you might as well be invisible.

The first round of the final four was almost a formality: We beat Tell City by 15 points, and across the bracket, top-ranked Kokomo High beat Logansport by 9 points. The final team between us and the championship was the state's fastest, deepest roster. Kokomo was loaded.

Kokomo is one of the more overlooked high school programs in Indiana history, but they were perennial state-title contenders in the late 50s and early 60s. In 1959, they lost a heartbreaker of a state final—two years before our matchup— and the 1961 team they fielded against us was arguably better, certainly one of the deepest rosters in the state. They ran a speed-centered offensive system rooted in strong rebounding, precise outlet passes, and layups on the fast break. They substituted new players in often to keep their legs fresh and their pace high.

Joe Platt was Kokomo's coach. He came to Indiana from a collegiate coaching position in Minnesota, and he brought a knack for recruiting and system formation with him. Platt used to go around to middle schools in the Kokomo area to teach the junior-high coaches his offense so when their players eventually came to his program, they'd be prepared to run the system. He basically built his own feeder-school network, so the Kokomo kids we faced had been indoctrinated in running the break, throwing the outlets, and hustling from whistle to whistle for years. They had it engrained in their muscle memory, to the point where the seniors on Kokomo's 1961 team had lost just three games in three years. These guys were Goliath, if Goliath could sprint.

At tipoff of the championship game, I felt the world shrink as soon as I stepped onto the court with my brother and the other Manual starters. The crowd's roar began to fade, the Kokomo starters came out to meet us, and it was like house lights around the arena had dimmed and there was nothing except the 10 players on the court, the ball, and the two hoops. None of us knew it, but we were about to play one of the most famous games in the history of Indiana basketball, the epic 1961 final between Manual and Kokomo. It would be the first championship game since the 1920s to go to overtime, and it would feature four future Indiana Basketball Hall of Famers. There would be enough swing points to make the crowd dizzy and more physicality than you could see on Fight Night. We were going to knock the shit out of each other. We'd swipe and claw on defense. We'd swat shots out of bounds. We'd run so hard we'd clutch our knees at the whistle. We were going to fall. We were going to fly.

Dick approached center court for the opening tip, and I lined up along the halfcourt line. Someone from Kokomo came to man up against me, and Jim Ligon, Kokomo's center, met Dick in the middle. Ligon was taller than Dick by three inches.

The referee brought out the ball, stood between my brother and Ligon, and held it out in front of his body. My brother set his jaw and crouched. Ligon crouched, too. The referee looked at one guy, then the other. He cocked his arm.

Across from me, my man pushed his forearm into my side. I pushed back.

The referee tossed the ball into the air.

***

The snow fell. I looked out the bus window, and it occurred to me I hadn't said anything in a long time. My mind was still on the game, the blown lead, Kokomo's go-ahead free throws with seconds remaining, the tiny margins that lead to our defeat. It was a deep, scarring event, like a war wound, and years afterward, I'd still be learning how much it changed people's lives.

The Kokomo game ended Coach Cummins' coaching career. He was devastated. He moved on to become a counselor in the Indiana public high school system, and after Dick and I made the pros, he was struck with severe heart failure. We visited him in the hospital, but even then, he couldn't stop talking about the final. He kept recalling plays out loud and bemoaning calls by the officials. He died during his attempted recovery. I wonder if it's possible to love basketball too much.

My father suffered severe side effects as a result of the Kokomo game as well. Like Cummins, he'd bring up what-if scenarios and ruminate on specific shots and calls. He had been living vicariously through my brother and me, chasing Indiana basketball glory for himself by way of our success, but after we missed out on it, his identity collapsed. Dad fell into an intense depression, and not long after, he was institutionalized in Indianapolis.

For all that my Dad felt after the game, he still didn't know how to process his emotions. He held onto things so tightly, and if those things hurt him, he'd just suppress them to avoid the betrayal. The only thing that gave him relief from this dynamic, actually, was Dick and me making the pros. Perhaps in his mind, reaching the NBA transcended the Kokomo loss and made up for the regrets he had about us. I feel bad he put himself through so much moral litigation. I never felt the same identity-bond to basketball, and it gave me a lot of peace later in life. There's a difference between regret and wishing things were different.

One of the blessings of my early career in basketball is I always had another opportunity. By my senior year at Manual, it was a given I would go with Dick to play for Indiana University. We even had scouts coming to talk to us about the pros. It was excruciating to bear the Kokomo loss in the moment, but it wasn't the end-all, be-all for me or my brother. We had a next.

But sometimes having a next is dependent on seeing you have one in the first place. Coach Cummins couldn't see his next. My father couldn't, either. The same might be said for some of my Manual teammates, regular old kids who grew with basketball but now had nothing in front of them, not even a chance to play in college. That's a confusing, empty place to be. Where do you go after that? How do you begin again?

I sat on the bus until I was alone, and I stayed there a long time. Soon, Sparky appeared up front and asked if I was alright. I said I thought so. Sparky told me everyone was waiting at the bonfire, if I wanted to go. I nodded. I stood up and walked past the rows of empty seats, and when I reached the front, Sparky gripped my shoulder. He didn't say anything else, and that seemed like the right thing to say. I tried to smile, and then I disembarked.

The bonfire stood in a wide, dark field. You could see the silhouettes of my classmates and teammates gathered around the flames, standing in circles and murmuring. A few had their arms around one another's shoulders. I saw my brother standing with some of our teammates, talking. One of the guys laughed. The wind picked up and the snow swirled and I put my hands in my pockets and started walking across the parking lot. My brother saw me coming, and he waved to me. I waved back, and I started jogging, headed toward the light and warmth.

***

Sixty miles north, the Kokomo team arrived back at their own school. They were late because all along U.S. Highway 31, a crowd had gathered in the cold to cheer as the team bus drove by. The players leaned out the windows and waved, and when the bus reached the school, it took another 15 minutes for the players to make it inside the gym—the fans had packed the place shoulder to shoulder. The local media was there, too. They peppered the kids with questions about the game and the comeback and what the win meant to the town of Kokomo. It was the basketball team's first and only championship in school history.

I met one of the Kokomo players decades later, at an event in Arizona. His name was Babe Pryor. Babe recognized me, introduced himself, and shared a memory he had from the game. He said he had tried to score a layup against me, but I had blocked the ball so hard it went into the crowd. To tell you the truth, I hadn't been too eager to talk to a Kokomo guy, but that story softened me up pretty good, and Babe and I ended up exchanging phone numbers. We're still good friends to this day.

Babe and his 1961 teammates are heroes in Kokomo. They give speeches at the local elementary school, attend honorary dinners during homecoming, receive free haircuts anywhere in town, and attract all kind of special treatment whenever they wear their class ring out and about. There's a mural of their team on the Kokomo High gym. It shows their starting guard, Ronnie Hughes, making the go-ahead free throws against us to give Kokomo the title. Dick's in the painting, tensing to jump for the rebound outside the circle. I'm not pictured. I was on the bench at the time, fouled out.

Before Babe, this was a simple story to tell: The good guys lost, the bad guys won, and life was unfair. It's never that simple, because life doesn't stop after its climactic moments. Aging complicates our stories. The bad guys become good. The good guys don't find redemption. Poetic justice never comes. This championship was the end of the road for many people, but for me, it was the turning of a page, the ending of one thing becoming indivisible from another beginning. That paradox was often difficult to grasp in my memory—for a long time, all I remembered about the Kokomo game was the loss I felt—but growing older, the phenomenon has clarified. Today, the more I think about the various endings of my life, the more I realize how many beginnings I had.

Chapter Four

This might be surprising coming from someone who played professional basketball back in the "old days," but my college experience was all about preparing for the NBA. I certainly studied hard—I was a major in economics and was even named a First Team Academic All-American at Indiana University, but I had no clue what I would do after graduation if I wasn't playing basketball. The sport was ingrained in me. It was the air I breathed. I wouldn't be satisfied in the world of finance, and even something like coaching basketball wouldn't have done it for me. Even at school, I wanted my life to center around running, jumping, and shooting.

That's not to say I—or my brother, for that matter—looked to treat college like a pit stop or an obligation like some of the guys in one-and-done programs today, but Indiana was primarily a place where I could shape my game. It was a training camp, almost, for my hopeful rookie season in the pros. I was still following a career path; it was just leading me toward basketball. Many college kids do the same with business or medicine or journalism, but I was lucky to be able to play hard as much as I studied hard. It was a heck of a lot of fun.

The recruitment process for my brother and me lacked a lot of the pomp and circumstance you find in modern-day high school athletics: Dick and I were dead set on going to Indiana, and we entertained pretty much zero alternatives. Of course, we had options—we shared the honor of Mr. Indiana Basketball our senior year, and that certainly garners you some national attention—but all the salesmanship and seduction young prospects enjoy today wasn't part of our experience back in 1961. There were no outlandish recruiting visits with parties and dinners, there were no gaudy gifts or envelopes of cash, and there was no National Signing Day where we had to sit in front of a row of microphones and put on a goofy-looking baseball cap (why do basketball and football players express their commitment with baseball gear anyway?). The most fanfare we saw in our recruitment process was a visit from University of Kentucky coach Adolph Rupp, who gave us a sales pitch in our living room, and a letter in the mail from UCLA coach John Wooden. I always thought that was nice of Coach Wooden, but let's be honest: He didn't need us to be Bruins. He had a revolving door of future pros at his program.

Even if Indiana University was a foregone conclusion for Dick and me, our decision surprised a few people. At the time of our commitment, Indiana was on probation from the NCAA tournament, and would continue to be until the beginning of our senior season. What high school player would want to go to school under those circumstances? Penalties like that still dissuade a lot of recruits—and in hindsight, I think Dick and I underrated how valuable it would be to earn some postseason experience in college—but I have a lot of grace for Dick and myself for making that trade-off. The NCAA tournament would have been an incredible opportunity, especially when you consider how my pro career turned out regarding the playoffs, but there's no way I could have known then how things would turn out. In the years since my time at Indiana, I heard a lot of what-ifs and woulda-shoulda-coulda from people around me—particularly my dad—about the alternative paths I could have taken if I had played for Kentucky or Ohio State or another perennial tournament school, but I don't chase those trains of thought. I was focused on preparing for the NBA, and the bottom line is few places would help me do that better than Coach Branch McCracken's Indiana Hoosiers. Now there was another man, like Coach Cummins at Manual before him, who believed in me and my ability.

Branch McCracken. That ringing, roll-off-the-tongue name still conjures a Pavlovian smile on every face in Indiana. Branch was the head men's basketball coach at Indiana University from 1938 to 1943 and 1946 to 1965, and he was nothing short of an icon. He won two national titles—one in 1940, another in 1953—and as a result it seemed there wasn't anybody in the world who didn't know his name and face. He had national fame, but like all the greatest Indiana legends, he maintained his local ties. He grew up on a farm in Martinsville, and he had an array of homegrown manners that, like a dominant power forward drawing double and triple teams on the low block, caused everyone in a room to move toward him. He could walk down any street in the state and strike up a conversation. He welcomed people's admiration and entertained all questions and compliments. If you ask me, he really earned the right to be cherished by the fans. People loved Branch and he loved them back. He was a hero to Dick and me, so to play for him was an honor.

Indiana University as a whole hadn't lost its mystique, even with the violations. This was the school my brother and I had watched on our neighbor's little TV growing up, and it was the place so many of our heroes—Walt Bellamy, Hallie Bryant, Don Schlundt, Bobby Leonard, Dick Farley, Archie Dees, Wally Choice—had furthered their careers. It was the Big Time for us. *We were going to play for Branch McCracken? We were going to be*

Hoosiers? It was another one of those childhood dreams come true.

They say never meet your heroes, but meeting Branch was a treat, and he was everything you would hope. He had huge hands and a grand handshake. He had basketball height (6'5" to be exact—I've found I have a skill for pegging people's height to the inch, which is probably a symptom of being a basketball player) and a handsome face and a powerful way of presenting himself. He leveraged his gravitational charisma to tremendous effect as a recruiter and coach; you'd follow him to the ends of the earth. No matter how good or bad our team was at Indiana—and we had our share of ups and downs—I was always sure we had a chance to win with Branch pacing along our bench.

Many modern coaches have earned bona fides through sideline tantrums in which they shout at officials and scream themselves red at players. Think of guys like Bones McKinney, the former Wake Forest coach who put a seat belt put on his chair to contain his antics. Those guys are a lot of show. Branch wasn't like that. He was more of a rah-rah motivator than a punisher. His positive reinforcement was well-suited to me in particular. I was an internal motivator. I always looked in the mirror and analyzed my performances for myself, so if you yelled at me, well damn it, I was just going to show you. Branch always said he'd rather recruits have that kind of inner dynamite than be passive and in need of a pep talk. As a coach, he could temper some cockiness, but he couldn't instill it if it wasn't there. I think that's true.

After Dick and I committed to Indiana as seniors, Branch went around telling people that was one of the greatest days of his life. That was special. He said he couldn't believe the two best players in the state had chosen to overlook Indiana's probation and forego three years of NCAA tournament eligibility just to play for him. You could tell it meant a lot to him, and to express that to the public struck me as uncommon and humble. It was a huge encouragement.

I think most athletes want coaches that make them feel free to embrace their gifts and play their style, as opposed to adapting to a system. Branch was eager to promote the talent he saw in Dick and me. We had quick first steps, decent speed and lateral quickness, strong vertical leaps (37 inches—I still remember), and more aggression and toughness than most could handle.

Our final year at Indiana, our team started the season 9-0 under the strength of a full-court press defense. Branch placed Dick and me as the two frontcourt defenders, so it was our assignment to corner the man who received the in-bounds pass. This individual would usually be a smaller, faster ball-handler, but Branch trusted Dick and I could leverage our athleticism to stay on him. It was a savvy coaching move that, in consideration of how modern NBA teams hybridize wings and seek out "tweener" players who have the speed to cover guards and the size to cover bigs, was pretty ahead of its time. In those days, it was unconventional, but Branch knew we could handle it. He was far and away the best thing that happened to me prior to the pro game because he emphasized the attitude, work ethic, fundamentals, and pure basketball skills that made a good professional. To this day, I can't thank him enough.

Branch had an attitude of service toward his players, as if we were doing him a favor by entering his program. I remember one time at school, Dick and I were laid up sick at our fraternity house and Branch came over himself with bags full of groceries he thought would help us feel better. He had sacks of oranges and chicken noodle soup, all kinds of things. It was really sort of fatherly of him. Can you imagine John Calipari or Bobby Knight doing the same for their players? I love Coach Knight— we're good friends—but during his coaching days he would probably be more inclined to accuse a sick player of faking an illness so they could wriggle out of doing wind sprints rather than hand them a tablet of vitamin C.

This general way of being for Branch definitely had an impact on our roster and how we related to each other as teammates. It was a good tone-setter for the rest of my career. Branch assembled most of our team from local Indiana players, so I knew many of my peers by reputation before we played together. Some of them I had competed against in the state tournament, and others I had encountered on the Indiana public courts during pickup games. Our freshman season, Dick and I were teammates with Jon McGlocklin, Steve Redenbaugh, Al Harden, Ron Pease, and Ron Peyser—all local stars in their hometowns—and while this meant we shared a reverence for the Hoosiers program meant and for Branch, it also meant there wasn't any obvious team chemistry when you looked at our roster on paper. I hear stories about modern college players and pros meeting each other in AAU tournaments and club leagues, and it feels like a whole other sport compared to the way the amateur system worked in my era. In the 1960s, your school was your primary basketball community, so whenever you graduated to another level, you were always starting from scratch when it came to your coaches, teammates, and eventual friends.

That idea—from-scratch teambuilding—was going to play a major role in my NBA career, it turned out. I'd join so many different rosters with so many different personalities I now see it as a strength that I couldn't pick and choose my teammates growing up. I really believe part of why Indiana prepared me so well for the pros was because it taught me how to be friends with anybody, regardless of where they came from or what role they played on the team or...heck, even what racial background they had (in those days, some guys still saw this difference as an obstacle in the locker room, and that was a great challenge).

Race ended up being a recurring theme over the course of my professional career. That might sound strange coming from a Midwestern white man, but people in the 1960s were conscious of race in a more explicit way than people today, I think. The national dialogue at the time about segregation, integration, inclusion, and equality was such that everyone had to decide how they related to those things as individuals. Of course, black players in places like the NBA often didn't have a choice about participating in this dialogue—my friend Oscar Robertson has many stories about times when his race was twisted into a weapon against his dignity regardless of his will—but among white players, guys had the freedom to be involved in the conversation (on one side or the other, mind you) or keep it at arm's length and—in the parlance of modern media—"stick to sports."

For Dick and me, participation in the basketball world's racial dialogue felt natural, almost inadvertent. Growing up in farm country, we didn't have the most diverse upbringing—there was maybe one black family in all of Johnson County—but the first time I remember thinking about race in a sense of differentiating one person from another was when Mom and Dad took my brother and me to Crispus Attucks to watch their basketball team when we were kids—Attucks was the all-black school in Indianapolis, of course.

Attucks had some amazing players—many of whom became our heroes—but outside of idols like Hallie Bryant and Oscar Robertson, I didn't have many preconceptions about race in general. I guess the homogeny of Greenwood meant most people didn't have to talk about it. As a kid in the 1950s and '60s, that was probably for the best, considering the alternative mode of discussion in many parts of the country.

In high school, Dick and I had played with a few black players at Manual. The competition in Indianapolis exposed us to all kinds of different backgrounds through our opponents, too, and looking back, I know that was valuable. What stands out to me more, though, was how this dynamic didn't feel particularly special or unusual at the time. My brother and I didn't really give this kind of diversity much thought, if only because it felt so normal to be a in a place where white people were getting along fine with black people. In fact, I remember the sectional tournament during our junior year was marked by such a bad snowstorm the roads to the arena were closed and we had to hunker down in somebody's house near the gym. I ended up rooming with one of our black teammates, Roger Wood, and though I realize now plenty of people back then would have raised an eyebrow at the situation, it wasn't anything significant to me or to him. Roger was my teammate and I was his teammate. That's just the way it was.

Over time, however, those unconscious actions became a little bit more intentional, especially during the Indiana summers. Dick and I were good enough to be influencers in the Indiana basketball scene as teenagers, and that meant the pickup scene revolved in part around where and when we chose to play. Back then, pickup was kind of like a network. My brother and I would tell some of our friends we were going to play in, say, Beach Grove that night, and word would spread and by evening all kinds of kids would be pulling their cars into the Beach Grove parking lot. Black kids, white kids, rich kids, poor kids, kids who'd gone deep in the state tournament the season before, and kids who couldn't even dribble with both hands. The court became a cultural blender. All guys wanted to do was play.

A few courts, however, have become rather historical in the years since Dick and I ran in the pickup games. Indiana Avenue had an all-black YMCA on it, and the games on their courts were particularly competitive because they operated on King of the Court Rules. You entered with a random group of guys, played 5-on-5, and kept playing with that team until another team beat you. Then you had to sit out and wait until it was your turn again. Oftentimes at that YMCA, Dick and I would be the only white players. I don't remember being singled out at all, but we must have stuck out. After all, there are still times when people recognize us from those games: "Hey Van, how you doing!" That's fun.

We all related to each other just fine at those courts, and I think that's the sign of a true basketball community. Dick and I went up there because that's where we knew the best players in Indiana were competing—race didn't even factor into our heads—and as a result we built some cherished, sustained relationships. I suppose we just saw guys for who they were, and that wasn't a common mindset back then. Honestly, I'm not sure it's a common mindset today. I think some of the ways we've progressed as a society have been really positive, but every so often I find the modern attitude surrounding race—the kind of hyper-awareness people have toward their differences—to actually be counter-productive to us just treating each other like human beings. When Dick and I went to the Indiana Avenue YMCA, we knew we were the only white guys, but we behaved like we belonged because we were basketball players and the other guys were basketball players, too. We had no fear. And they embraced us.

When people today talk about not knowing how to act around black people, it kind of frustrates me, because when you think about how you're "acting," you're not being normal and you're not approaching others on a person-to-person basis. There were times in my pro career when I moved teams and had to walk into new locker rooms with new teammates and coaches and assert myself as someone who just fit right in with everyone else. It was the same dynamic as the pickup courts. I couldn't be performative or posturing, because guys could see right through that. Seeing everyone as a person first and foremost is the key to being a great teammate.

I understand on some level that in the days of my youth, racist rhetoric must have been present in my environment, but I wonder why it didn't pervade my consciousness. I suppose nowadays you can find evil, divisive language without even looking for it. Cable news is explosive and hard to ignore. Stereotypes are common in movies and TV. Backwards thinkers can find fame on social media and other places online. Even newspapers have op-ed sections that seem more designed to incite anger than initiate productive dialogue. When I was growing up, these outlets for negative discourse either didn't exist or weren't as prevalent. Remember: Dick and I had to go to our neighbors' houses just to watch TV sometimes.

And as celebrities of a sort, modern professional athletes are asked to enter this discourse more than players were during my career. The most outspoken athletes of my era discussed things like race and integration because they actively wanted to move the conversation forward, not because they were asked to comment. Oftentimes, my peers took on race relations in a way that strikes me still as profoundly sacrificial. Oscar Robertson and Bill Russell took enormous strides—and often suffered awful repercussions—to progress our nation's attitude about race. Oscar has told me, and has written about, numerous stories in which he was outcast, rejected, hated, mistreated, or targeted for nothing but being black. Those stories really shake me, but they've been some of the most valuable things I've discussed with another pro. When guys like Oscar and Russell stuck their necks out for the things they believed in, there were real consequences on the line. It's a different world today, where Nike embraces political athletes and men like LeBron James and Dwyane Wade are celebrated for their activism. Not many people were clapping for Oscar's criticisms of American society in the 1960s and '70s.

One thing I recognize that is similar between the modern guys' way of being in respect to race and politics, and the pros of my era, is that within the world of basketball, guys feel safe to take those stances among their teammates. I'm not sure it's always the same with coaches, owners, and other executive personnel, but when it comes to your peers in sports, it really is a fraternity, and really is a place where guys have this kinship and sense of loyalty that allows them to be 100-percent themselves. That's special.

I'm 77 now, and with the (sometimes limited) wisdom that comes with age, I believe our world would be a much better place if people treated each other with the mutual respect athletes have for their peers and opponents. Some of the pros today assume tough guy stances and mug in each other's faces, but sports still carry an undercurrent of dignity I think would be instructive for the rest of the world. Why else do you think athletes are so quick to hold each other back when altercations break out on the court? Guys know they're setting an example. In my era, picking a fight with Wilt Chamberlain was like a basketball death sentence, but whenever someone was foolish enough to do so, it wasn't their teammates who stepped forward to put a lid on things, but Wilt's teammate Al Attles. If someone made a move at Wilt, Al would run over to Chamberlain and throw his arms around him in a giant bear hug, anchoring him to the ground and keeping him from escalating the fight. It wasn't about protecting Wilt—the big man could definitely handle himself—it was about protecting the opposing player. As soon as Wilt felt Al grab him, he'd back down. Those guys were competitive, but they weren't hostile. The context around them, the game of basketball, placed demands on their behavior. I think many sports work that way.

The pickup games in Indiana were my first taste of that solidarity and camaraderie, and those things saw a natural extension during the four years I spent in college with my brother and our teammates. Basketball 50 years ago had these built-in systems—formal and informal—to foster fellowship among the players. Our community games were as diverse and active as any professional sports environment today (except the amount of foreign-born players; that's come a long way in the pros), but the biggest difference is how often we saw the same guys over and over again. By the end of our time with the amateur scene in Indiana, Dick and I knew we could call up Ron Thomas from Shortridge High to come play with us, Bill Jones from Crispus Attucks, a couple more kids from Cathedral High—"Everyone good to meet at Cathedral's gym tonight at 6:00?" *Sure thing. I'll be there. Let's do it*—it was organic.

Today, the game is such a big business, and I think it affects how players interact. Some guys will play club or AAU together—Indiana actually had a famous AAU team in the 2000s featuring future pros Greg Oden, Mike Conley, Daequan Cook, Eric Gordon, and Josh McRoberts all on the same roster—but those systems allow you to choose your situation so precisely that it's rare guys stay in one place very long and build real relationships, in my opinion. Plus, the college game today is hardly more than a minor-league system for the pros. The one-and-done rule encourages guys to treat college like a pit stop rather than the full experience I had at Indiana, and I think that's a huge loss.

More than anything, I remember that dirt court Dick and I ground into our backyard at our home in Greenwood. When we were in high school, we turned that into a hub for local pickup games itself. We'd host players from all over the county and from as a far as Indianapolis to come down and play with us. We installed a light so we could play at night. We had the two baskets up. Our parents would come out in lawn chairs and watch the action. It was idyllic. Guys would carpool in and park out front and walk around back and we'd divide up the teams and play our asses off. We put out the hose for guys to drink from during water breaks. I'm telling you; Norman Rockwell could've painted those games. They were really something.

The more I see what's happening in the world, the more I believe we as athletes showcased unity in a really forward-thinking manner. It's a good example to the rest of society, and pros from my era all the way to today really emulate it well. You see black guys and white guys hugging all the time, joking around, slapping each other's backs, celebrating big plays. And many of them didn't even have the high school or college camaraderie I shared with my peers. That's just the power of sports, of showing up to work with someone and striving toward the same goal alongside them day after day. I'm proud of that example.

A lot of kids in Indiana had the same dreams I did; they grew up longing to play professional basketball. Everyone wants to be in the NBA. But I think to really survive in the pros, the NBA has to want you back, and that mutual acceptance can only come from sportsmanship, compassion, and a willingness to see the pros as a fraternity of men, not just a place to collect a paycheck or show off your talents.

I can think of some great individual players who only had marginal success in basketball. Each of them could do things most NBA players, let alone me, could only dream of doing, and yet they had difficulty throughout their careers finding a home in basketball because they were so difficult to connect with in the locker room. They isolated themselves, criticized their peers, and put up walls. Their stat lines might have been impressive, and they might have competed for a few playoffs and Finals teams, but even considering the lowlights of my luckless career in basketball, I'm not sure I would trade my experience for any of theirs.

I made lifelong friends in the NBA. I gained perspectives I'd never have otherwise. I met my heroes. I turned my dream into my everyday life, and for huge stretches of my career, it really was that dream come true. Were there disappointments and frustrations along the way? You bet. But I built a career because I made a point to treat every locker room like an opportunity to make friends, take on leadership roles, and be a positive influence. More than the money or the thrills or the tiny piece of fame I enjoy now, that's the most valuable thing I took from professional basketball. The NBA wanted me around. I'll always be thankful for that, especially considering how during my first few weeks as a professional, I almost fled from the game altogether.

JOURNEY MAN

Chapter Five

Ray Scott had a beautiful home, that was for sure. Earlier in the week, our starting forward had invited the rest of the Detroit Pistons over to his house for dinner. This was common on our team—guys had each other over all the time, usually when we played extended homestands or had a day off before going back on the road—but Scott was a veteran, and it felt like a big deal for the rookies on the team, me included, to be included on a night like that.

Scott was our second-leading scorer my rookie season in 1965. He averaged almost 18 points per game and nearly 10 rebounds. He was in the heart of his prime, 27 years old, four years in the pros, and one of those NBA guys who could find a way to serve just about any team he played for— "a pro's pro," as folks in the media might say. He never made an All-Star team, but he averaged double-digit points his first 10 years in the league. He was a role model for the young guys.

I showed up to Scott's house with one of my rookie-season roommates, Ron Reed. Ron's second season in the NBA would be his last—he jumped to Major League Baseball in '66 and ended up pitching 19 seasons in the bigs—but we're still good friends. Even back then, he was my buddy, and as a couple of rookies, we knew we had to stick together. It was nice to have someone looking out for you when you had dinner with all the vets.

It ended up being a typically fantastic night at Scott's house. There was lots of lively talk, plenty of jokes and laughing, good basketball debate (we're jocks—did you expect us not to discuss sports?), and some great food. Well, for the most part.

Professional athletes can sure eat, and in those days, we didn't exactly have the nutrition guidelines and know-how the modern pros do today. We took care of ourselves, but heck, this is when guys were still smoking cigarettes in the locker room and eating steaks the day of a game. Plus, every time we went on a road trip, the team would give us money for meals. We were used to eating well, is my point.

Anyway, when Scott had the team over for dinner, he would set out the food buffet-style in the dining room. This wasn't no early-bird buffet, either. Scott had the caterers—that's right, caterers! —put all the entrees and sides in great silver dishes so the food could stay warm and everyone could help themselves. Ron and I made our way down the line, helping ourselves to greens and potatoes and cornbread.

As Ron and I neared the end of the buffet, our teammates filed out ahead of us to go eat in the other room, and it was just me and my roommate left helping ourselves. As Ron nudged some casserole over on his plate to make room for yams, I opened the last silver dish.

"What's that?" I said.

Ron peered over. The dish looked sort of like tiny chicken parts. Ron frowned. He picked up the little card in front of the dish. "Chitlins," he said.

"What are chitlins?"

"I don't know. They look like chicken wings though. Scoop me some."

I took the big serving spoon and heaped a mound of chitlins onto Ron's plate. "Woah," he said, recoiling just a little.

"What?" I scooped myself a big helping of chitlins. As soon as they plopped onto my plate, mixing with all my potatoes and gravy, it hit me: a smell unlike anything I had experienced before. It was different, alright.

I raised an eyebrow at Ron. He grimaced and glanced at the door. "Hurry," he said, and he took his fork and tilted his plate and slid his chitlins right back into the serving dish. I saw some yams follow close behind.

With a quick look over my shoulder, I scooped back my chitlins and replaced the spoon and closed the lid. Ron reached over and moved my cornbread, so it took up the empty space on my plate. He nodded. "We better get in there," he said.

We headed into Ray Scott's dining room. At the head of the table, the 6'9", 215-pound power forward saw us enter and smiled. He gestured to some empty seats. "You rooks take some chitlins?" He beamed. Scott really was the nicest guy.

Ron beamed back as we took our seats. "Shit, Ray, I'd be shocked if there was any left for you."

Scott chuckled and winked at us and turned to talk to Dave DeBusschere. At the other end of the table, Ron and I laughed into our napkins. After coming up for air, we tucked into the food on our plates. It really was delicious. I swear.

***

I don't think modern players have as much fun as we did in the pros. These days, it seems everyone in the NBA has their own personal group of friends from their hometown or high school or college, and they usually are spending time with them rather than their teammates and coaches. On one hand, I understand why. The game is a business now, and that means players are more likely to view each other as coworkers rather than family members. On the other hand, acquiring a sort of second family in the NBA was the best part of my experience in the pros. Really, it's the reason I stayed in the pros. I loved my teammates like brothers, and the lessons and stories I took from our time together are really the heart of this book.

Reflecting on my time as a rookie in particular, it's impressive to me how the veterans embraced us first-year players. Here I was coming in from little old Greenwood to play with guys from Detroit and New York City and Philadelphia and all kinds of places, and they never brushed me off as the hick country kid or the corn-fed farm boy. Nope, I was just Van. That made it easy to acclimate to all the new faces and places I was seeing; like having a tour guide for every city we visited, and a friend everywhere you went.

One of the most well-connected players in my draft class was Billy Cunningham. Billy was a good player. He was a part of the 1965-66 All-Rookie team with me, my brother, Rick Barry, and Fred Hetzel, but he went on to have a Hall of Fame career. He won a championship with the Philadelphia 76ers in 1966-67, and when he made a brief jump to the ABA in the early 70s, he won their MVP award in 1972-73.

Billy and I had played together in something called the World Games after both of us had graduated from college (he attended the University of North Carolina), and across six weeks of playing in Budapest and other places in Europe, we had become close. Any time you could see old friends and teammates of yours on the road, you did it. We really were this great community.

But Billy was a gregarious guy. He had grown up in Brooklyn, and as soon as he made the pros, he became one of the go-to individuals who could help us connect with restaurant and bar owners in the city. He just loved using his network to bring people together, and it seemed he had good friends outside the pros no matter where you went. Most of the times I traveled to New York to play the Knicks as a pro, I could count on Billy for suggestions on where to go, where to spend my walking-around money, and who to name-drop for a table or a barstool. It was great.

When I entered the league, the Philadelphia 76ers were perennial championship contenders. Wilt Chamberlain was their obvious star—he won the MVP award my rookie season—and they had guys like Hal Greer and Coach Dolph Schayes as overqualified supporting-cast members, so to speak. I remember the first time my Detroit Pistons met them in competition in 1965, it was an exhibition game before the official season began, probably somewhere out in Hershey, Pennsylvania, or another small town where the NBA was trying to stage a showcase and promote itself. There was very little special treatment in those days, so when me and the Pistons and Billy and his Sixers stepped off our respective planes (normal, commercial airliners—there wouldn't be charter flights in the league for a long time), we walked to the baggage claim together to collect our luggage.

63

It was great to see Billy. "Hey Van, how you doing?" He clapped me on the shoulder and smiled. We talked for a minute about training camp and the travel, before Billy gestured over to his teammates: "Hey, come meet the guys."

Of course, at that point I was still a wannabe rookie; I hadn't officially made the Pistons roster yet. So, any invitation to even stand with a group of real-live NBA players was a treat, let alone to stand in a circle with Wilt Chamberlain, one of the greatest players who ever lived.

Wilt was a giant. He stood 7'1"—well over my 6'5"—and weighed 275 pounds in his prime. Just massive. I was awestruck in his presence, but whether it showed on my face I'll never know, because Wilt the Stilt put on no airs around me and he shook my hand as if we were peers. He fit right in with the rest of us, from role players to bench guys to kids like me and Cunningham who hadn't even made the team yet. We all stood around laughing and catching up, but of course, Wilt was a superstar, and superstars have a tendency to command a conversation even if they don't intend it.

During a pause in our chatter, Wilt asked the group if we'd like to see a photograph of his new girlfriend. Now, I'm well aware of Mr. Chamberlain's reputation with women today—as well as what he's said about his, shall we say, prowess—but back then, I was just a naïve little kid. Everyone in the group said sure thing, Wilt. He reached into his pocket and took out his wallet and retrieved a photo.

The picture was of a beautiful blonde lady. Wilt handed it to the guy next to him and we started passing it around the circle. Guys raised their eyebrows and grinned and handed it along and all the while Wilt told us about her and where she spent her time and how he had met her. He had a huge smile on his face. The picture came to me and I took a closer look. The woman really was fine-looking. She had long hair and long legs, a nice smile, and atop her blonde head was a graduation cap with a little tassle hanging over the side. To go with that cap, she had on spiky high heels and a sparkling gold bracelet, and apart from that, nothing else at all. I blushed and handed the photo to Billy. I looked at Wilt. His grin was almost as broad as shoulders. What could you say?

***

My first year in the pros took me on a tour of meeting and playing against all the stars I had admired as a kid. It was pretty mind-blowing for me to compete against people like Bill Russell, Oscar Robertson, Sam Jones, and Jerry West, and even after I had made the Pistons roster and secured a spot in the league, I always caught myself wondering what the hell I was doing playing against these guys. It's funny now to think about how those guys must've seen me: a young, naïve, scrappy kid in some respects, but in other respects, still an opponent they had to outsmart and outplay and outhustle.

One of the dreams I had always had of being in the pros was playing in the Old Boston Garden. It carried a sort of romance about it—a museum-like, cathedral-esque atmosphere—and I imagined playing there would be like playing in the Church of Basketball. When the Pistons made our first trip there my rookie season, I could hardly wait. This was going to be like Butler Fieldhouse on steroids.

Well, it was like that for the most part—at least when you were playing the game. The rest of the experience at the Garden wasn't much different than a Motel 6.

Even back in the 60s, the Old Boston Garden was ancient. It was musty. The visitors' locker room was gray, drab, full of roaches, and the showers only had enough hot water to tease you with a comfortable spray before they ran icy cold and you had to hurry the heck up. It was awful then, but compared to the luxuries of the modern game, I bet today's players would vomit at the sight of those locker rooms. At the very least, they'd file a lawsuit.

We used to hear rumors that Red Auerbach, the Celtics coach at the time, requested the visiting team's facilities at the Old Boston Garden be neglected just to create discomfort for his opponents and give the Celtics more of a home-field advantage. I'm not sure if it worked quite like that, but I'll say this: Visiting the Old Garden was like walking into an Edgar Allen Poe story. It was spooky. You wondered how many bodies were hidden beneath the cement.

And yet I will also say, jogging out onto that arena's famous parquet court and feeling the wood beneath your sneakers was like nothing I could've imagined at all. It was better. We were each like Moses, running around on holy ground. Every piece of wood had its own feel. I didn't have this kind of savvy as a rookie, but over the course of my career, dozens of visits to the Garden translated to an exacting knowledge of that court. You learned the dead spots where the ball wouldn't bounce. You learned the springy spots by the basket where you could sky for a rebound. Certain parts of the floor felt like they radiated little zones where your jump shot was especially pure, or little spots on the glass that always seemed to deflect the ball right toward the hoop. It was a special place, and I have to add this: I always seemed to play well when I was there.

Of course, the other factor in the Garden's mystique was its hosts. Auerbach was his own kind of celebrity, but first and foremost in my mind as a rookie were the Celtics stars. You had the all-timers—Russell, Sam Jones, K.C. Jones, and John Havlicek—but then you had three more future Hall of Famers on the bench: Tom Sanders, Don Nelson, and John Thompson. Does it go without saying the Celtics won the NBA championship my rookie season? They won the Finals eight out of 10 times across the decade, and the 1965 title was their eighth in a row.

Of all their clout, no one was more regal, more dignified, more awe-inspiring than Bill Russell. Allow me to be the thousandth person to put it in writing: Russell was a hell of a player, and a hell of a man. If I were assembling a team from players throughout history, he's my first pick without question, a true winner (and for the record, Oscar is my second pick— sorry, Michael).

The first time I visited the Garden as a rookie to play Boston, I saw some minutes. I don't remember how I played, but I do remember a couple of foul shots quite vividly. I wasn't shooting the ball. I was down on the blocks preparing to go for the rebound. Across from me, on the other side of the lane, were Bill Russell and Sam Jones, maybe the greatest pair of teammates ever. I was almost struck dumb I was so starry-eyed. I should've known better. Bill Russell saw me looking at him. And he smiled.

Bill Russell's smile contains multitudes. It's a beautiful smile, but it's knowing, and cunning, and disarming. When he deploys it, you feel like you've known him 1000 years, and you feel like you should kneel in his presence. He's regal. When he smiled at me, I almost felt my knees start to shake.

"You're having a pretty good game, rook."

I didn't know what to say. Sam Jones saw Russell looking at me and chimed in: "Yeah, you're really not bad, kid."

Bill Russell and Sam Jones were complimenting my game! I couldn't believe it! Did I realize later they were only doing this to distract me and throw me off? Yes, I did. But still, it was pretty darn cool. If a couple of legends feel like they ought to trash-talk you a little, you must be doing okay. And maybe I did tighten up a little after that, but hey, that's the game of basketball for you. Eventually, I would play Russell and Jones and Havlicek so many times that going to the Garden was just another day at the office, but don't let anyone tell you that meeting your heroes like that at first is just routine. It's not. Even the Celtics' peers in those days knew they were great. Heck, the Celtics themselves knew they were great, and they leveraged that greatness to their advantage.

There's one more Boston story. It was my third year with the Pistons, and we were battling with the Celtics throughout the first half. Late in the period, I called for a pick and roll with our backup center George Patterson, a 6' 8" rookie. Patterson had some size to him, and he planted his feet near the top of the circle, and I took a hard step around him, keeping my body close to his to knock off the defender.

The pick worked great. I cleared George and cut to the basket, keeping the ball on my right side and reaching my left arm out to space myself from the defense. I felt my arm hit something, but I still had a lane in front of me and I drove hard and finished at the hoop (the shot went in—I remember that). As soon as the ball found the net, I turned around to hustle back on defense. The Celtics were known to be the best fast-breaking team in the league, and it was important to go back and spot your man.

But as I was running down the floor, something didn't feel right in my left arm. It was so strange I stopped running and looked. There, in my left forearm, was a front tooth. A big one, just dangling there.

I couldn't believe it. I looked back up the court to see George bent over with his hand over his mouth. You had to be kidding me. I hurried over to him and he saw me coming and he moaned and tilted his head back and pulled his hand away. One of his front teeth was gone and the other was hanging from his gums. There was blood all over the place.

Obviously, they stopped play right about then.

George and I both went back to the locker room for treatment. Him for, well, his mouth, and me for the gash in my arm. The medical staff at the Garden sutured my wound so I could play in the second half—and no joke, I did.

Things calmed down after the game. I showered and dressed with the team and we headed to Logan Airport for our flight home. My arm was aching during the trip and the flight, but nothing too alarming. I made it back to my apartment and to bed no problem, too.

But then, around 3:00 in the morning, I woke up from my sleep and realized something was wrong right away. My arm was in a thick bandage and I unwrapped it to see that from just about my elbow to my fingertips, my arm had swollen to about twice its normal size. I looked like a horror-movie monster. The skin was puffy and shiny and the sutures from the locker room were starting to pull at my skin. It hurt like hell, and it was damn creepy.

I took myself to the Ford Hospital Emergency Room, my heart going like a crazy man.

In the ER, the attendant doctor identified the cause of the swelling right away. Apparently, the person who treated me at the Boston Garden had sewn some of my arm hair into the wound when they sutured it shut, and what's more, the gash hadn't been cleaned properly after George's lost tooth had cut me and infected my arm. The ER doctor gave me some shots of antibiotics and some meds to take down the swelling, and I recovered just fine, but gosh, it was a scary moment. I never thought Red Auerbach would strive to the lengths of medical sabotage to take out an opposing player, but hey, I guess now we know. (I'm kidding.) (Sort of.)

Truth be told, for me and many of my peers in the NBA at that time, there was something really aspirational about those Boston teams. Their posture toward winning was—despite how often the victories came—always reverent and respectful. Some might say Red's victory cigar reeked of elitism, and maybe it did a little, but in my mind, it's as much an acknowledgement of how special it is to win in the NBA as it is an act of gloating, perhaps more so. Walking off the floor after a thumping at the hands of the Celtics always brought mixed feelings. Their fans had a haughty attitude and their personnel wallowed in each win, but you couldn't shake the sense that those guys really cherished the game of basketball. Winning was always special to them. I'd rather a team treat each armful of victories like that than take them for granted. Red Auerbach and that dynasty are a significant part of NBA history. I always wished I could have been a part of one of those great teams.

***

These days, the internet and social media have made criticism of the pro game much easier to come by than praise. It seems even the great modern players are always a little overrated in some fashion, or a little imperfect in another fashion, and all manner of role players are nitpicked to death by analysts and fans online. Let me join my fellow NBA alums in saying this: Every professional basketball player who built themselves a career in the pros did so for a reason, and at the heart of that reason is the simple fact that they are very good at basketball.

When I played in the NBA, the league was much more consolidated than it is now. Detractors of the old game say the fewer number of teams made it easier for guys like Russell and West to make the Finals year after year, but I propose the concentration of talent should raise the opposite expectation. Every night during my time with the Pistons, it seemed we had to tangle with a couple future Hall of Famers, a championship contender, or a roster of All Stars. Even our team—the worst in the league in 1965—had two future Hall of Famers on it, and multiple All Stars. The Knicks, only one spot above us in the standings, had three future Hall of Famers. The clout of the Celtics and Lakers in those days goes without saying. There were no nights off, and with the more intense schedule and worse accommodations, I'd argue we had it much tougher than modern guys, who play in an era of diminishing back-to-backs and this frankly baffling concept called "load management." I can't really imagine any of my coaches giving me the night off while I was healthy. Playing basketball was my job, and I was going to do it every chance I had! Sure, sometimes I'd feel the grind of a season—if you go back and search through our old game logs from the 60s and 70s, you'll see it wasn't unusual for us to play 8 games in 10 days—but that was just part of my NBA dream. I loved playing. That passion carried me through some of the tougher stretches of the season.

And for a rookie in 1965, the NBA was an intense gauntlet of talent and ability. On one night, I might've been matched up against a wily veteran like Richie Guerin—I'll tell you a story about him later—or sharing the court with one of my childhood heroes, such as Oscar Robertson (he'll have a whole chapter to himself). It was one of the treats of my rookie season and beyond to find that, as I matured into my career, the star power of the NBA greats never diminished, even as I came to know many of them on a personal level. That's one of the beautiful little social elements of sports. Competition humanizes everyone, but at the end of the day, you never lose a sense of who the really incredible players are. You can look up to people and be their friend for life. Sports facilitates that sort of mutual admiration.

***

Before the start of training camp, I still had to prove myself to the Pistons. Not long after I was drafted, I joined my fellow rookies in Detroit to acclimate to the team and introduce myself to the veterans—or, more accurately, allow the veterans to introduce themselves to me. Their ideal way of doing this: a good old-fashioned scrimmage.

Fans can't imagine the tension involved when you are competing for a spot on an NBA team. It raises some complicated emotions. On the one hand, I really enjoyed many of my fellow rookies—including my future partner-in-crime Ron Reed—but on the other hand, I was chasing my lifelong dream. I couldn't step back and be polite and let another guy through. In my mind, I wasn't a sure bet. I had to work for my spot.

Ray Scott—it always seemed to be him who roped me into these wild scenarios—made the invitation to the rookies to join the veterans for an informal scrub game. Of course, you want to impress the real pros, so we all said yes, and so we were all matched up and given our defensive assignments. I had the pleasure of being matched up against Eddie Miles.

I didn't know Eddie Miles from Adam at the time, but my rookie season he'd be named a league All-Star and he'd lead our entire team in scoring—just a hair shy of 20 points per game. He was 6'4", 195, which is the kind of height and weight combination you feel more than you see, as I soon found out. I had spent summers at Indiana University working as an iron worker, and as far as I could tell there wasn't much difference between Eddie Miles' forearms and a #10 rebar. This guy was tough, and solid, and for me, totally immovable. I don't know if he was actively trying to gauge my skills or test me in the scrimmage, but I just couldn't drive around him, and he barely allowed me the space to shoot, if at all. On the other end, he drilled shots over me like I was a mannequin.

Turns out, professional basketball players are pretty good.

The biggest step from college ball to the pros is strength and aggressiveness. Of course, a professional's experience allows him to process the game faster and make better decisions, but aggression helps a guy make those decisions with assertiveness and speed. And strength is correlated to capability, plain and simple. The stronger and tougher you are, the more you can do on the court. The more you can use and set screens and be involved in plays, the more you can finish around the basket and score, the more you can grab rebounds in traffic, the more you can draw attention from a defense and pass out of the shift. Strong players impose their will on the court. That's why guys like LeBron James are so good. They bully everyone else around; they literally make other players move out of the way so they can do what they want (the officials' favor doesn't hurt, either).

And if you don't have the perseverance to develop strength and aggressiveness, you're not going to make it in the NBA. There are two Indiana legends, Rick Mount and Jimmy Rayl, who were absolutely terrific in high school and college, but didn't do anything in the pros, and I believe that's because they didn't have the perseverance to improve when the NBA knocked them around a little. A lot of guys don't make it for that reason. Think of all the recent young college players who were picked high in the draft—Bennett, Thabeet, Fultz—who wilted when it came time to actually play. Those guys just never improved.

When I watch pros today, I can still tell who has those special ingredients. I can tell by their energy—the way they attack a defense or guard an imposing player—and by their general effort. Modern guys talk so much. I'd rather just see them hustle.

Now, I was a skilled player, no doubt about it, but after that scrimmage against Eddie Miles and the veterans, I knew I had a long way to go. It was my perseverance that helped me overcome those early deficits and succeed and build a long career. I wasn't an All-Star right away in the pros, but I had the work ethic and the determination to make myself one.

To think that before all of this happened, I almost gave up.

***

Dave DeBusschere serves as the bookends of my career. He was there at the end, when we both served on the board of the Retired Players' Association, but he was there at the beginning, too. DeBusschere was my first coach in the NBA, and he's the person to whom I owe probably the most important second chance of my life.

When I was drafted to the Pistons and my brother was chosen by the New York Knicks, it occurred to me that it would be the first time we would be apart. Dick and I always figured that would be the case—to think otherwise would have been unrealistic—but the reality of living day-to-day without my brother and best friend alongside me hit much, much harder than I anticipated. At the time, I'd say I was terribly unhappy moving to Detroit and preparing for training camp alone. Now, I'd say I was depressed.

There's an important difference between being sad and being depressed. When you're sad, it feels like...well, a feeling. It's temporary and manageable and you can do things to change it, like call a friend or take a walk in the sun or put on a song you enjoy. Being depressed is not like that. When you're depressed, it feels like you can't change it, and you can't see the other side of it, and so you reach a place sooner or later where you think you have to take an extreme measure to escape your depression.

For me, that extreme measure was to leave the Pistons and go back to Indiana—for good.

I had a backup plan all along: I had been accepted into law school in Bloomington, so I decided I'd quit on the NBA and go be an attorney. On the fifth night of training camp, I told my roommate, Rod Thorn: "Rod, if you wake up in the morning and I'm not here, it means I left to go back home." Sure enough, Rod woke up the next day and I was gone.

I went home to Greenwood. My mom was there, and when I told her what my plan was, she didn't chastise me or question me. She just said: "Okay Tom. Think about it and make sure this is what you want." Dick called me from New York. He was in better mental shape than I was. He wasn't like Mom; he said I was making a mistake. I couldn't see what he saw. I just saw how lonely I felt and how uncertain I was about life on the Pistons. I drove down to Indiana University and bought all my law books and registered for classes. It was a Thursday (I still remember that), and classes began on Monday.

I found housing with my cousin Ole, who was a pre-med student, and after moving in with him, I cracked open one of my new books to prepare for my first day. The subject still burns into my mind: *How to brief a case.* The words reached my brain, but they didn't excite me at all. All of the synapses and sparks and inspiration I felt when I was passionate—when I was playing basketball—were quiet.

Oh my God. What the hell am I doing here?

I called Dick. He had been phoning me every day urging me to go back to camp. "Dick, you were right," I said. "I need to give myself a chance."

Dick was fired up.

"You think Coach DeBusschere will take me back?" I asked.

My brother paused for a second. "Well, have you asked him?"

Could you even ask something like that to a professional basketball coach? I wasn't sure. I figured if I was a coach, and any of my players had ditched the team in the middle of the night, I'd be upset to the point of no return. But it was worth a shot. The NBA was worth it. I said goodbye to Dick and called Coach DeBusschere.

He answered. "Tom?" I wasn't sure if he was surprised.

"Hi Coach."

"What can I do for you?"

77

"Coach, I'm down here in Indiana, but I don't want to go to law school after all. I want to be a Detroit Piston. I want to try to make the team. I'd like to come back to camp if you'll allow me another chance."

Dave DeBusschere was a thoughtful, kind man, but he was very direct. "Tom, you can come back to training camp on one condition: You don't ever do something like this again. We're a team of professionals. That means I need your full commitment and your full effort. You're all in, or you're all out."

I nodded on the other end of the phone. "I understand, Coach. I'll be there. Thank you."

"Thank you, Tom."

DeBusschere was a man of few words, but he was perfect for me. During my rookie year, he was a player-coach, the youngest coach in NBA history, in fact—just 25 years old. But he was mature beyond his years. He knew what it was like to be a player, and he knew what an adjustment it was to go through training camp. His instinct made it easy for him to earn your respect.

And hey, you know, he must've thought I was pretty good. Otherwise he would've told me to stay in Indiana. Most rookies have little moments of doubt when they wonder whether they can make it in the pros, but funny enough, after DeBusschere invited me back, I had a new confidence. It was a sign he wanted me to contribute. As I said before, the NBA has to want you back for you to build a career.

***

One of the things I'm most proud of and encouraged by in regard to today's game is how the players discuss mental health. Depression is awful. It's worse than being physically hurt or injured. You can't be talked out of it, you can't tough it out, and you can't just "get over it." All you want is to not feel alone and to be listened to. My mom was good at listening. So was my brother Dick. DeBusschere, in his way, was good at it, too. Each of those individuals might have disagreed with my decision, but none of them made me feel like I was crazy. That's so important, and I think in the NBA today, you see players share a similar kind of empathy.

For fans, it's easy to look at pro athletes and ask, "Why would they have any reason to be depressed?" We're blessed with money, fame, attention, and the gift of playing a sport we love. But when guys like Kevin Love or DeMar DeRozan go public about their anxiety, depression, panic attacks, whatever it is they struggle with, it empowers their peers to speak out and destigmatize those issues, but also care for them better as teammates. For me, when those guys speak out, it means the world. It reminds me I'm not alone. It reminds me other people—even other pro athletes, with even more accolades and honors and championships than me—have experienced what I have. It's come a long way.

I came close to missing my dream, but I had a support system around me that was ahead of its time and gave me the grace I needed to come out of my depression and make a reasoned choice about my future. That's a rare opportunity. I had two chances to play professional basketball—two chances to experience all of those memorable team dinners, trash talking, freak accidents, and welcome-to-the-NBA scrimmages—I didn't waste the second one.

Some would say I am pretty lucky.

Chapter Six

The NBA landscape changes on a year-to-year basis, and if I knew then what I know now, I would've been ready for all the changes in Detroit between 1965 and 1967 to impact my career. In the moment, I was blind-sided. I had no idea what was coming.

The Pistons improved from 22 wins to 30 during my second season in 1966, enough to encourage management to invest more in team development to try and lift us into the playoffs. Dave DeBusschere was still our coach in my second year, but he had to balance those leadership responsibilities with his on-court play: He was our defensive anchor, minutes leader, rebounds leader, and second or third scoring option. It wasn't tenable for him to serve both roles. Player-coaches weren't meant to be long-term solutions anyway; they were stopgaps. The Pistons' front office wanted to establish their next chapter under a more permanent figurehead.

So, toward the end of my second season, the Pistons brought in Donnis Butcher as Dave DeBusschere's replacement at the head coaching position. Donnis was a night-and-day difference from Coach DeBusschere. Dave was cerebral and thoughtful, known to lead more by example than vocalization, but Donnis was a classic old ball coach. He was from the Appalachian town of Pikeville, Kentucky—the kind of place where you're raised to chew on dirt and shit bricks—and it was his manner to stick his finger in your face and tell you exactly what (he thought) you needed to hear. I don't have a problem with that style, but it wasn't my preferred way of developing as a player, and while I have no disrespect for Coach Butcher even to this day, we never quite clicked like DeBusschere and I had.

In fact, I had a history with Donnis Butcher prior to him coaching the team. He was my teammate on the Pistons during my rookie season, and he's actually at the center of one of my "welcome to the NBA" moments, the kind of initiation story every athlete seems to experience.

When I arrived back at training camp after my sojourn to Indiana Law School, I had decent hopes of making the Pistons' roster, but there were a few veterans between me and one of the primary guard positions, one of which was Donnis Butcher. Donnis didn't have the talent to be a starter in the pros, but he had an intense work ethic and a competitiveness honed from several seasons of fighting off upstarts like me for playing time. He was determined to make his living playing basketball, even if it was only for 15 or 20 minutes per night.

That's how most guys in the NBA have to build their careers. Becoming a professional athlete changes your relationship to your sport in a significant way. You're still playing for the joy of the game, but there's an added urgency of having to maintain your status in order to keep doing what you love. As players, we're independent contractors alongside a host of other people trying to attain the same things we are. That means there are winners and losers, haves and have-nots. Once the pecking order is established—starters, reserves, and so on—the team crystalizes and everyone can work toward a collective goal, but even then, you maintain your individual interests. You have to look out for yourself, or you'll lose your place on the team.

This dynamic creates and informs the politics around playing time, or what players refer to as "PT." Donnis wanted his 15-20 minutes of PT, but as a rookie, I wanted some of that PT, too, and since there are only 240 available minutes per game across a basketball team's five positions, that PT comes at a premium—you have to take what you can. This makes training camp tremendously stressful for guys like Donnis—bench players at risk of losing their minutes to a newly acquired player or a touted incoming draft pick, like me in 1965.

So Donnis and I were battling for minutes at the guard spot in training camp. We were family on the Pistons, but enemies for PT.

It was an early scrimmage at camp, and a defensive rotation matched Donnis on me in isolation. I had the ball. My ball handling was decent, but I had my trademark physicality and aggressiveness, so I gathered a head of steam and drove on Donnis toward the basket. He stayed with me, body to body, but I had a trick up my sleeve. I reached out with my non-dribbling arm and hooked him around the waist, locking him down and allowing me to spin off of him toward the hoop. With Donnis clear of my hip, I was able to make the basket and finish the play, but it seemed Donnis still had a little more action in him.

As I turned to go back down the court and play defense, Donnis grabbed the arm I had hooked around him and pulled me to a stop. I skidded on the floor and looked back at him. Donnis drew himself up right into my face. "Rookie, if you ever do that again," he growled. "I'm going to break that arm right off your body."

Now, I was a few inches taller than Donnis, but my gosh, did he seem to tower over me then. I told him yessir and shook my arm free and ran back down the court. I didn't harbor any hard feelings—competitiveness is something you learn to live with in pro sports—but it was an apt first impression of the player Donnis was and the coach he would become. He was defensive, set in his ways, and unafraid of anyone or anything.

Donnis took over for Dave DeBusschere with eight games to go in our 1966-67 season. He inherited an up-and-coming young roster lead by our latest number-one draft pick, rookie Dave Bing out of Syracuse. Bing earned our starting point guard spot right away in 1966. He led the team in scoring that season and was the NBA's Rookie of the Year, too. (Ultimately, Bing made seven All-Star teams, three All-Pro teams, and the Hall of Fame across his 12-year career—though he never won a championship.) It seemed Pistons management wanted to stack the backcourt around Bing, so in the 1967 draft, they took Jimmy Walker out of Providence College first overall. Walker, in turn, came aboard with guard/forward hybrid Terry Dischinger, who was returning to the Pistons after two years of military service. What's all this mean for Tom Van Arsdale? It meant I had a lot more guys coming for my PT than Donnis Butcher that season (though maybe I should've worried about him, too).

To make a long story short, I suppose Donnis wanted to take his guard positions in a different direction than my style. He cut my minutes to 16 per night in 1967 compared to 27 per night in 1966. It was disappointing. I spent most of each game on the bench cheering on the starters, though when I did see the floor, I did my best to hustle and give 110 percent. I'm proud to say my statistics that season, on a per minute basis, didn't

84

drop in any significant way. In fact, the numbers indicate I was probably a little more aggressive than usual; I had an extra foul per 36 minutes.

I don't resent guys like Butcher, Bing, Walker, or Dischinger for cutting into my minutes. That's just the way it goes. I was still a young pro, and I had a lot to learn about finding my place on a team.

A strange memory sticks out to me when I think about that period. After Terry Dischinger returned at the beginning of the 1967-68 season, we roomed together at camp. He was another Indiana guy—he went to Purdue—so we found we had a lot in common. We became pretty comfortable with one another. Now one night during camp, Terry and I were preparing to go to sleep when he asked me, "Hey Van, could I ask you a favor?"

I was changing my shirt and not really paying attention. "Sure Terry, what do you need?"

"Could you rub this on my feet?"

I stood up straight and turned to my roommate. Terry was sitting on his bed and he had kind of a sheepish grin on his face and he was holding up a little tin of ointment. I raised my eyebrows at him. I wasn't sure what to say.

Terry laughed. "I'm sorry, Van. It's been a while since I've played, and I'm developing some blisters on my feet. I'm not used to the shoes yet." He held up a foot. It was blotched with several shiny, red spots. "Normally my wife helps me put this cream on and it takes away some of the irritation. I know it's a little weird, but do you think you could give me a hand? I'd put it on myself, but it stings a lot, and it helps if somebody else does it."

And that's when I surprised myself: "Absolutely Terry, I'll help you after I wash my hands." And I did. I went over to Terry's bed and sat down next to him and applied ointment to his blistered feet. Terry winced and flinched at some of the pain, but when we were done, I could see the relief on his face. He clapped me on the shoulder. "Thanks, Van. You're a good teammate."

It's hard to explain the paradox of emotions you feel when you have interactions like this with your family members on the team. Terry was my brother on the Pistons. He was my friend. At the same time, he was taking some of my PT that year. He was my competitor. In a less healthy environment, we might have been called rivals. I had plenty of reasons—maybe even a good reason, considering the NBA was my livelihood—not to help Terry and gain an advantage over him, but that just didn't occur to me. Reflecting on this story, it strikes me how vulnerable it was for Terry to ask me for help in the first place. It showed a lot of trust, and I have tremendous respect for anyone who can approach someone with a request like that. I'm proud to say that despite what happened to our PT on the Pistons that season, Terry and I are friends to this day.

Despite all the changes happening on the team, the first half of the 1967-68 season started out well for the Pistons. Bing took a leap in his sophomore season to become the scoring champion of the NBA, DeBusschere thrived away from his coaching role, and across the roster we had seven players average double-figure scoring numbers. It felt like our team was forming an identity. Headed toward the All-Star break, about 50 games into the season, we had almost as many wins (26) as we had the entire year before (30), and we had more than in my rookie season altogether (22).

However, it looked more and more like that new team identity didn't have much room for me. I was still a gutsy player and I still thrived driving to the rim, but we had a lot of players who could run the floor and pass out of the lane, and a few of those guys were better shooters than me (it took a few years for my jump shot to really develop in the pros). Coach Butcher reduced my minutes more and more. I should've seen it all as a warning sign.

We were on the road in Philadelphia when I received a call in my hotel room from Coach Butcher. He wanted me to come see him in his room, so I went over. You're never sure what to expect in those situations, but that day, I knew whatever Coach had to say, it probably wasn't good. I knocked on the door and Coach answered. "Come in, Tom."

Coach Butcher always played it real straight. After I had stepped inside his room and closed the door, he gave me the news: "Tom, you've been traded to the Cincinnati Royals. They expect you to be there for their next game, and your flight leaves in a couple hours. When we're done here, head back to your room and grab your things."

I actually felt my knees buckle. I swayed. I'm not sure what I said, or if I even said anything. I was just in total shock. I had friends in Detroit, great teammates, a decent apartment, a social scene—I was going to have to start all that over again? The next day—well, really that night—I was going to live in another city, working for a new team under a new coach with a new roster of players. What would that look like? I didn't know much about Cincinnati beyond what I saw when we traveled there for road games. It's strange to know you're headed toward a new part of your life, but you can't imagine what that life looks like.

Coach Butcher stuck out his hand. "Thanks for all your effort, Tom. Best of luck to you."

His voice sounded like it was coming through an old radio. I barely heard it. I shook Donnis' hand, left the room, and two hours later boarded a plane to Cincinnati.

***

I worked in a pre-free agency era of the NBA, meaning outside of demanding a trade, pros had zero control over where they played (those trade demands weren't often successful, either). Once a team drafted you and you signed a contract to play for them, that team had complete control over your rights. If your contract expired and another team made you an offer to play for them instead, your original team had the power of "First Refusal," so they just had to match the competing offer to keep you. Teams could trade players, but those transactions were negotiated solely among management. We athletes didn't have any say in the matter.

This could sometimes be frustrating as a pro—you'll see I was on the unfortunate side of a few different trades—but in light of the free-agency luxuries modern players enjoy, it must sound like a prison sentence. Things like unrestricted free agency, no-trade clauses, and other wrinkles of the current Collective Bargaining Agreement make the transaction processes of my era look restrictive and disempowering. At the time, it made for some volatility and instability, but we didn't know what we were missing, and we just felt lucky to be playing basketball for a living. The NBA didn't have the global reach and cultural impact it does today, and that meant the players didn't have the same type of leverage. I envy the modern guys who can hold out on teams and manipulate their way into better markets or on to more competitive rosters. I don't always agree with those decisions—Big Threes in my time were built, not bought—but heck, would I have used those privileges to lift myself into the playoffs once or twice? Probably.

In my era, the fate of your career was dependent on the whims of team management. This made for some unpredictability, but in all honesty, I never thought of my owners and GMs as malevolent overlords. They were actually kind of oddball characters.

Fred Zollner was the owner of the Detroit Pistons during my two-and-a-half seasons with the team. He was of the basketball old school even in my day—he actually founded the Pistons, originally called the Fort Wayne Zollner Pistons, with his sister Janet in 1939—and he was pretty well-liked and respected among the fans, coaches, and players. The Western Conference championship trophy is named after him today. Anyway, you hardly ever saw Mr. Zollner during my time with the Pistons, so when his name came up not long into training camp my rookie season, it felt like guys were talking about a man behind the curtain, or some other mysterious figure.

We were in the locker room after a workout when somebody spread the rumor that if you made the Pistons' final roster, Mr. Zollner was going to buy you a new Chrysler car, complete with a little gold basketball hood ornament. I just couldn't believe it. Ron Reed and I looked at one another and grinned. We just had to make the team now; we wanted those cars!

Ron and I both made the team, but a few games into the regular season, there was still no follow-up word on the Chrysler cars. Someone finally asked DeBusschere about it, and he said he'd check for us. He went to go find Mr. Zollner, and he returned about 10 minutes later.

DeBusschere stood at the center of our locker room. "Guys, I asked Mr. Zollner about the Chrysler cars."

We all gathered around. *What'd he say, Dave?*

DeBusschere put his hands on his hips and frowned at the floor. "He said he changed his mind. No Chrysler cars."

No Chrysler cars?

"No Chrysler cars."

It felt like someone deflating a big balloon in your chest. Guys were so disappointed, groaning and muttering and giving little "Well, what can you do?" shrugs. And that was it. We were all a little more wary of Mr. Zollner's promises after that. Well, at least until Christmas.

My rookie season, we played a Christmas Day game in Los Angeles against the Lakers, and before tipoff there was another word from Mr. Zollner—except this time, Mr. Zollner gave the word himself. The Pistons owner appeared in the locker room as we're preparing for the game. He had a warm smile and a cheerful coif of hair and a big box tucked under his arm. He called us all over and when we were all giving him our attention, he let out one of those beaming smiles that wealthy guys always seem to use when they're about to show how generous they are with their money. "Boys, I have a Christmas present for each one of you."

All the guys shared a look. *What was this?*

Mr. Zollner opened his box and inside were these fine premium leather wallets. He passed them all out. The wallets were dark and rich and shiny and, my gosh, you could really smell the leather. A couple of my teammates opened their wallets up, and when they saw what was inside, they gave a little smirk or a chuckle. I opened my wallet, too, and tucked inside was a crisp $5 bill. You just had to smile. We were making five figures, but hey, not bad! Everyone thanked Mr. Zollner, and he thanked us right back for making the Pistons proud. We took the floor of the Los Angeles Sports Arena just a few minutes later, full of the Christmas spirit.

The Lakers beat us like a drum. Jerry West, their superstar, scored 44 points, while a couple of our key scorers went cold. I actually had a decent game—18 points, 9 rebounds, 5 assists—but there's no joy in that when you lose. Back in the locker room after the game, it felt like the furthest thing from a holiday.

Then our general manager, Ed Coil, stepped into the room. Ed wasn't as popular as Mr. Zollner. He didn't have any experience with basketball before taking the GM job, so whenever he was sent in to do management's dirty work, he didn't exactly keep himself clean.

"Men," Ed announced. "Mr. Zollner has instructed me to tell you that in light of today's performance, and in light of the Christmas present he gave you before that performance, you will each be fined $100."

We couldn't believe it. Really? A couple guys shouted in disbelief and threw towels, but mostly you just saw eye rolls and exasperated faces.

Ed Coil was quick to leave. But when he reached the locker-room door, he hesitated. He turned around. "Merry Christmas, men."

And no kidding, $100 was missing from my next paycheck. How do you like that?

***

It's still hard for me to view the NBA as a business—I was paid good money to play my favorite sport, and that's just too lucky —but my experiences with Mr. Zollner and my moments on the trade block remind me that owners and GMs have to consider their bottom line as much as the livelihood of their players or the success of their team. It's sobering. You're reminded that you're an asset, sometimes just a name and number on a budget sheet, and if your number doesn't suit the man balancing the books, you're expendable. It makes me a little uncomfortable framing it that way, but that's how it is.

The mechanics of player transactions in my era meant you were really lucky if you landed on a team that prioritized winning as much as it did earnings. Think about it: There are tons of great players in the free agency era to never win a championship—Charles Barkley, Karl Malone, John Stockton,

Chris Paul, Steve Nash, Reggie Miller, Patrick Ewing—and they could theoretically play for whatever team they wanted. In my era, there was less mobility, and more concentrated talent. Elgin Baylor made eight NBA Finals with the Lakers and never won a title. Pete Maravich never won one, either, nor George Gervin nor Bernard King nor Nate Thurmond nor Dave Bing nor Connie Hawkins. Every single one of those guys is in the Hall of Fame, but none of them won an NBA championship. It's really difficult to win, and I think we forget that too often when considering a player's legacy.

A guy like K.C. Jones comes to mind for me when I think about this point. K.C. played for the Boston Celtics for nine seasons between 1958 and 1967. He won eight championships in those nine years—amazing—but he never averaged double-digit points in a season, never shot above 40 percent in a season, averaged 4.3 assists and 3.5 rebounds for his career, and only logged more than 30 minutes per game in four of those nine seasons. I have a ton of respect and admiration for K.C. as a competitor and professional, and he was apparently a heck of a teammate, but his numbers aren't Hall of Fame numbers by any stretch. He never made an All-Pro or All-Star team! But he's in the Hall of Fame.

My point is: Situation often begets success in the NBA, and that means there are athletes whose success (or lack thereof) isn't reflective of their real ability. Now, I know part of my opinion on this is motivated a bit by self-defense—I never was lucky enough to play for a playoff team, let alone a championship team—but I'm passionate about the way NBA players are remembered. I think a lot of guys aren't remembered as well as they should be because they were stuck in unfortunate circumstances. And gosh, I sometimes sure wish my own circumstances had been different!

One of my favorite NBA players to talk to about the game is Tom Chambers, who became the first unrestricted free agent in NBA history when his contract with the Seattle Supersonics expired in 1988. Under the new Collective Bargaining Agreement, Chambers was able to choose his next team, and he signed with the Phoenix Suns. It was a revolutionary change for basketball players in general, and it worked out well for Chambers—he made three All Star teams in Phoenix and averaged over 20 points per game as a Sun. When I ask Chambers about his experience with and views on free agency, he explains that beyond the money and opportunity, free agency gave him the flexibility and freedom to find where he best fit among the other pros in the NBA. He could sell his scoring ability as a power forward and go somewhere that specifically was looking for a man of his talents. When he went to Phoenix, he was slotted in the starting lineup among point guard Kevin Johnson and spot-up shooter Jeff Hornacek, and further, he was put in a staggered rotation with guard/forward Eddie Johnson, the Suns' first option off the bench. It was a perfect fit. Chambers lead the team in scoring and rebounding during his debut season, feasting off passes from K.J. and never clashing with Johnson. That kind of cohesion is possible now with free agency. It's very fortunate.

So, to me, modern free agency is a bit of a mixed bag, even with the obvious advantages Chambers outlines. I envy the guys who can go where they want and join healthy organizations and leave toxic environments—I sure wish I had those opportunities—but I think that mobility has come with some entitlement. I felt lucky to be competing at every stop of my

NBA career, and even during some of the least successful seasons any player has ever been through, I never took the opportunity to be a pro for granted. I think guys today do, just a little. They're too easily dissatisfied. My attitude always was: Make the best out of whatever situation you're in. Guys today are just thinking about the next thing. That's probably one reason why they flip teams so often.

And absolutely, it stings a little to see great players like LeBron James and Kevin Durant find success so easily because they can join rosters with other Hall of Famers—I wish I could have done that! But I don't think it's fair to compare the legacy of a guy like Durant with a guy like Oscar Robertson. Durant had the freedom to choose where he played; Oscar, never.

This is all to say that being traded to Cincinnati raised a lot of thoughts for me I had never considered about what it meant to be a professional athlete. My life was changing around me, and all I could do was react. I couldn't anticipate anything. I couldn't plan. I woke up thinking I might live in Detroit for years to come; I was staring down a new job, a new city, and new friends just a few hours later. Boarding that flight to Ohio, I still had a little bit of that weak-in-the-knees feeling I had when Coach Butcher gave me the news.

But as I walked down the aisle through first class toward coach, who should stop me but George Allen, then the head coach of the Los Angeles Rams football team, and now a Pro Football Hall of Famer.

"Van! How you doing?"

I looked twice—it was really him. "George Allen! How are you? You know, I'm okay." I let my voice drop a bit. I usually tell people exactly how I'm feeling.

George frowned. "Just okay?"

This was a fellow sportsman. He was up on the NBA, so I could be honest. "I've been traded from the Pistons to the Royals. Coach Butcher told me this morning."

"That's a tough thing to be traded. What's your take on Cincinnati?"

"They have a decent team"—my mind went to one player in particular— "so it's not all bad, but it's a lot of change. Makes you feel a little strange, you know? Just to be let go."

George shifted in his seat so he faced me a little more. "I understand that, Van. But you know something? I think about this—sometimes being traded is the best thing that can happen to a player. It might be the best thing to happen to you."

"Really?"

"Sure. Think about it this way: The Pistons don't want you anymore—that's a tough pill—but on the other hand, the Royals do want you. They look at you and your skills and your style and they say, 'You know, this guy has a place on our team. Let's see if we can pick him up.'" George shrugged. "Not so bad when you think about it like that."

Huh. I hadn't thought about that. I smiled and stuck my hand out. "Thanks, George."

The coach beamed and shook my hand. "Best of luck to you, Van."

I walked back to coach, feeling a little better.

***

I was traded several times, and I was always treated well by my new teams. Cincinnati did a fine job of greeting me and introducing me to the city and to all the team personnel. A representative with the Royals met me at the airport and, since the team was playing a game that night, took me to the arena so I could situate myself in the locker room and find a place on the bench to watch and support my new teammates. I was looking forward to seeing the guys—remember, I had competed against most of them already. We all sort of knew each other, and one of the guys I actually knew pretty well.

The team was expecting me when I entered the locker room, and they all welcomed me and shook my hand. The representative facilitated the introductions, and we worked our way down the row of lockers from one man to the next.

Then, toward the back of the room, I saw him. I could hardly believe it. When Coach Butcher had given me the news of the trade that morning, the first thing I thought of was how shocking it all was, but the second thing I thought of was this particular player. Maybe George Allen was right. When I saw this player in person, a grin took over my face and I felt myself stand up a little straighter. This was happening.

"Tom, have you met our team captain?" The team representative lead me over to where the man was seated in front of his locker.

I stepped forward. "I sure have."

The Royals' captain stood up and smiled at me. His hand came out and clapped into mine. *Thwack.* I felt a surge of energy. He said: "Welcome aboard, Van."

I almost laughed I was so excited. "Good to see you, Oscar."

I was on a team with the Big O. It was Oscar Robertson.

Chapter Seven

Even though we shared a backcourt in Cincinnati, I don't think I was ever in the same universe as Oscar Robertson. He was my idol growing up, my idol as a professional, and is still my idol to this day. He's the kind of person you strive to emulate even though they have things you will never attain, or even understand. Oscar's world was and is far from my own, his manner is unlike anyone's I've ever met, and his abilities have never been matched. But the privilege of knowing Oscar lies in all of those differences. I didn't just play basketball with my lifelong hero; we became friends. I can hardly believe it still, and it is one of the honors of my basketball and non-basketball life.

My friendship with Oscar originated, ironically, in how little we had in common. We are both Hoosiers—he was born in Tennessee but moved to Indiana when he was quite young—though our experiences with Indiana diverged in almost every way imaginable. I grew up white in Greenwood, a place so homogenous I only had to think about race until other people pointed it out (which, in my house, wasn't often). Oscar, meanwhile, grew up black in Indianapolis, where he was forced to consider racial difference all the time regardless of his choices.

We were both Mr. Indiana Basketball—him in 1956, me in 1961—but while I was heralded for my character, work ethic, *and* talent (despite never winning a state championship), Oscar was only recognized through the stereotypes that sports fans and media still assign to black players. People said Oscar was an elite physical specimen, hyper-athletic, sometimes "stylish" or

99

"flashy," but they never acknowledged his intelligence, fundamentals, and reserved mode of leadership (often black athletes or leaders are described as "passionate voices" or "strong motivators," rather than as tacticians or strategists— which Oscar was). When Oscar led Crispus Attucks High School to back-to-back state titles in 1955 and 1956, the City of Indianapolis changed the championship parade route so his team, the first all-black state championship team in American history, was diverted from the public, bustling downtown and kept to the poor (read: black) areas of the city.

The differing ways the world saw Oscar and me even affected where we played college basketball. When I was deciding where to go to college, my path to Indiana University was always obvious—it never occurred to me I might not belong there—but Oscar says his recruiting experience at the school was demeaning. He chose to attend Cincinnati instead.

Oscar is one of the most preternaturally talented people I have ever known, but being black meant he had to work twice as hard for the chance to demonstrate those talents as white players. His road to the NBA was a gauntlet of social and political challenges, but once he arrived, he asserted himself as one of the best to ever play basketball.

The Big O's career accomplishments are almost too famous and numerous to recite: 12 All-Star teams, 11 All-NBA teams, the 1963 league MVP award, the 1960 Rookie of the Year award, a championship with the Milwaukee Bucks in 1971, a scoring title, and six assists titles. Most people know he averaged a triple double in 1961, but he also had averages within mere tenths of a triple double in 1960, 1962, 1963, and 1964. Oscar averaged over 25 points per game for his career—14 seasons in total—and averaged over 30 points per game in a season six times. He shot over 48 percent for his career, a mark I never hit even in one season. Hey, I guess the guy's pretty good!

I've shared about the first time I met Oscar—it was at that Indiana track meet where he smushed his hot dog to give me an autograph—but the first time I saw him was in grade school, when my father exercised his staff privileges at Emmerich Manual to take Dick and me to see some of the great Indiana high school teams in person. Our favorite team to see, far and away, was Oscar's Crispus Attucks Tigers.

The first image that strikes me when I remember Crispus Attucks is the color of their uniforms. It might sound like a small point, but the team wore these green and gold uniforms, and the color combination evoked some kind of royalty, like warrior-princes of the ancient world, or high-ranking military leaders. A lot of high school teams would take the court whooping and hollering—you know how kids are—but Crispus Attucks never did anything like that. They emerged from the locker room like a procession of soldiers, chins up, surveying the arena and their opponents like conquerors, as if the idea of losing wasn't just an impossibility to them, but something they'd never even heard of before. They were proud. They were a basketball dynasty. When I saw Oscar in the green and gold from my seat on the bleachers, I thought he looked like a king. I was in awe of the way he and the other Tigers handled themselves. Of course, I was blown away by how they dominated their opponents, too.

After Crispus Attucks had inevitably built up a huge lead, their cheerleaders would take the court at the beginning of the fourth quarter and do this cute little chant. I still remember it; it permeated my mind. They'd all stand in a line and shake their pom poms and shout:

"Are you *satisfied?* Are you *satisfied?*"

No gloating. No bragging. No obvious jab about the score or the victory. Crispus Attucks' play just spoke for itself. I never saw the team do anything disruptive or demonstrative. They came out, kicked everybody's ass, and went home. Knowing Oscar, it totally makes sense that some of his most formative years were spent in this type of culture.

Everything about basketball seemed easy to Oscar. When he was on the floor, the ball, the basket, and all the other players seemed to bend to his will. He was impossible to guard—I had to match up against him a few times during my Pistons days, and it was both a nightmare and a dream come true—and he was utterly unimpressed with every single one of his opponents. He had respect for guys like Bill Russell and Wilt Chamberlain, but he never played small or distilled his game against them. Russell in those days was a sentinel in the paint, a manned guard tower of insurmountable defense, but Oscar attacked him like a cavalry battalion—tall, fluid, graceful. Oscar had so much assurance in his game that the facts of who was on the other team didn't matter, and that was hugely impressive to me. I had never seen anyone play like that, as if their own success was a sure thing. It ended up being one of the best things for me to observe as a pro.

As Oscar and I became closer and I learned more about his experience away from basketball, I felt my early admiration of him grow more complex. Oscar's life was defined by struggle, and that made me feel fortunate to watch him excel on the court, the one place where he didn't seem to experience oppression. If anything, my intimacy with Oscar made his on-court achievements even more astonishing.

Although our difficulties on the way to the Royals were incredibly different, I suspect those respective challenges played a key part in Oscar and I becoming friends. Neither of us took anything for granted, and even though he was a surefire future Hall of Famer and I was still searching for my place in the NBA, we both fought endlessly to earn our accomplishments. That's essential to both our personalities.

Oscar and I didn't speak much before I joined the Royals—when our paths crossed, I was usually too busy trying to stay in front of him to chit chat—but soon after I arrived in Cincinnati, we began to find things in common. We first connected over being Hoosiers, which surprised me given Oscar's fraught relationship with Indiana. We talked about the old high school state tournaments, Crispus Attucks and Emmerich Manual, our old coaches, Butler Fieldhouse, and all the quirks of playing basketball in a place defined by the sport. Our first conversations were really just the two of us reminiscing. Remember that nasty old gym? Remember that sweaty old coach? Oscar had a bit of a grumpy side to him, and he loved complaining about the old days. He was funny. It intersected well with my cheer and open-mindedness.

But we started forming a true connection over family, which I'd say is probably one of the central elements of Oscar's life. He volunteered some information about his upbringing, but he was quick to ask me questions about mine. He asked often about my brother Dick—by that point playing for the NBA's newest expansion team, the Phoenix Suns—and was always curious how my mom and dad were faring back in Greenwood.

Oscar had two older brothers himself. His dad worked various jobs and his mom sang in their church's gospel choir. He'd tell me a few stories about playing street sports in his part of Indianapolis as a kid, or about how his first date with his wife Yvonne was at a Carmen McRae show at a Cincinnati nightclub (she admits that during the intermission, they did talk a little basketball—I became close to Yvonne as well). I always enjoyed these stories, but Oscar was reserved about his past. It took a long time for him to share the whole picture of his life before the NBA; to this day, family history and well-being is still a tenant of our phone calls and catch-ups.

One thing that's always been special to me: The first question Oscar always asks me whenever we catch up is, "How's Dick?" My brother had a stroke in 2005, and ever since he found out about it, Oscar has been keeping tabs. It means the world to me.

As our knowledge of one another's personal lives grew, Oscar and I began to spend more time together on the road. Traveling with Oscar was a heck of a lot of fun, although I admit sometimes it was at his expense. Sometimes on the plane between games, he'd fall asleep with his mouth open, and as all the other guys watched, I'd try to dangle a cigarette from his lips without waking him. When Oscar would grunt and start to wake, I'd snatch my hand away and he'd open his eyes and swat out the cigarette and whirl around in one of his classic Oscar huffs. *Hey! Who did this?* We'd just howl. Every now and then, the Big O would catch the joke and chuckle at himself, too—a rare sight.

Oscar and I roomed together on road trips after my first year with the Royals. We'd kill hours and hours in the hotel talking about all things basketball, debating the best players, who was overrated and underrated, which coaches we'd want to play for, and generally arguing and gossiping our way through the whole NBA landscape. Some people might think it's a little weird that two basketball players would just sit around and talk about work all day, but come on—we were jocks! Basketball was our world, the main thing we had in common, and we never felt self-conscious about it. We still discuss the game today. Oscar has plenty of opinions, still, about new players and old players and how much the game has changed, some of which I'm sure would surprise anyone… but those are just between us pros.

Talking with Oscar about basketball was an effective way to both learn more about him and realize our common ethos about the game and about life in general. Oscar has specific ideas on what makes someone a good teammate, coach, or person in general, and I'd say both of us have a knack for judging people's character. We have acute noses for bullshit, and when we smell it, we don't tolerate it.

Oscar has a curmudgeonly reputation among his contemporaries. He was known in our day as an extreme, ultra-demanding perfectionist, and that label has stuck to him with age. I saw Oscar's intensity—I saw him yell at teammates and argue with Bob Cousy, our coach—but from my perspective it's too simplistic to put that behavior in the same category as other "difficult" behaviors you read about from pro athletes. Oscar was a savant, and he ran into the same problem many savants do, where they don't quite understand why the things that come easily to them don't come easily to other people. When Oscar saw you make a mistake on the basketball court, or be overmatched by an opponent, his experience told him you just weren't trying hard enough—after all, if he ever made a mistake or was outmatched, he could always just correct the issue with a little more effort. He didn't know about "couldn't," because he could do anything. Failure to him was always a matter of effort and execution.

Here's an example: During a game my second season on the Royals, we were playing a specific rotation that saw me and Oscar in the backcourt and Connie Dierking at center. Connie was a vivid guy. He was a spindly 6'10", with flowing blonde hair and a dapper grin, kind of like if you flattened out a Beach Boy with a rolling pin. Everyone liked Connie, even Oscar, but in this particular game Connie became a little lax on defense. The other center was just eating him for lunch, and not long into the game, Connie's sincere contests at the rim became a little half-hearted, a classic case of a player trading defensive effort for more offensive juice: "If you're gonna get yours, I'm gonna get mine." Well, Oscar began to notice this from Connie, and you could see it was nagging at him.

After yet another basket from the other team's center, our very own Brian Wilson lookalike began shuffling up the court again to take his spot-on offense. Oscar was bringing the ball up, and as Connie trudged by him, Oscar said: "C'mon Connie. You're letting that guy make moves all over you. Let's see some hustle!"

Connie heard that, straightened up, puffed out his chest, looked over his shoulder at one of the greatest players of all time, and said right there with the eyes of God and the team and the whole crowd upon him: "Aw *fuck* you, Oscar!"

We almost had to take a timeout everyone was laughing so hard. I completely forgot my position on the play, the other team's defense sagged, and both coaches were shocked into a standstill. I think even Oscar was a little surprised; that was something a lot of guys might have wanted to say to him at one time or another, but no one had ever had the guts to do it, and perhaps Connie knew he was so well-liked he was the only one who could actually get away with it. And believe it or not, there were not hard feelings between Connie and Oscar after that, but it was a rare dismissal from the Big O. Normally, the deal was if you wanted Oscar to pass you the ball, you'd better be nice to him, and listen to what he tells you (he was usually right, anyway).

Even with the criticism against him, I maintain Oscar was the best teammate I ever had. He did more for my confidence as a basketball player than anyone else in my career. As a leader, he didn't do much speechifying or pep talking to motivate you, but he set a rigid example by his perseverance and work ethic, and he expected you to match his intensity. Fortunately for me, I shared that ethos with Oscar, and that meant when he had a note on something I could do to improve my game, I always took it with the right attitude. When he told me to flare out to the wing on a fast break, I did it. When he told me to make a back door cut, I did it. When he told me to set a screen or box out or clear the lane so he could drive, I did it. He was Oscar Freaking Robertson, and he knew best. Not many NBA players have shared a backcourt with one of the greatest of all time. I figured I better take all the help I could.

Oscar saw my willingness to learn, so he rewarded me with opportunities. You realized you had Oscar's trust when he passed you the ball in a crucial moment. That was an incredible feeling. During one game in the 1970 season—my second full year with the Royals—we were on the road in San Francisco against Jerry Lucas and Jeff Mullins. I had been trading swings with Mullins the entire game, and Oscar had been giving me every look I wanted (it was an unusually deferential night for Oscar, he had "only" 19 points on 13 shot attempts, with 10 assists and 6 rebounds). The score was tied 119-119 at the final possession, and Oscar was bringing up the ball for us one last time.

I was in the off-guard position—small forward in modern terms—and as we transitioned into our offense, I spied my spot on the floor—right of the circle, about 20 feet from the hoop—and keyed Mullins, who was guarding me. Oscar was bringing the ball up the left side, looking for an open man. I cut toward the top of the circle as Oscar shaded to his left, drawing the defense toward himself and opening up the rest of the floor. I lost Mullins. Oscar saw me break open. I reached my sweet spot, planted my feet, and extended my hands for the ball.

And Oscar sent the pass. Right in the pocket. I brought the ball up straight into my jump shot and buried it over Mullins' belated block attempt for the win. It was sweet. I led all players in scoring that night with 28, but I was most elated that Oscar demonstrated his trust in me during a game-deciding moment. He had the ability to take any final shot he wanted, but he trusted me to shoot that one. And I delivered! It felt like I could do anything.

Sometimes Oscar had to take on a more explicit leadership role, beyond just setting an example and doling out his trust. My first year in Cincinnati, Ed Jucker was our coach. He was a college-hoops veteran who had coached Oscar at the University of Cincinnati (Jucker led the Bearcats to back-to-back NCAA championships right after Oscar left, in 1961 and 1962). Ed was a fine man, but he always looked more composed than he was. He had a ready smile and wore the heck out of a suit, but in tight games he'd be as nervous as a Billy goat, pacing the sideline and fidgeting, folding and unfolding his arms. During one particular home game, we weren't doing so well, and Ed—whose skin was almost clamming up before our eyes—called for timeout. We all entered a huddle.

In those days there were no crowds of assistant coaches or water boys in the huddle. It was just us and Ed. Our coach put his hands on his knees. He looked around, trying to organize his thoughts and sputtering. "Uh…uh…" His eyes darted over each one of us. They landed on Oscar. "Oscar!" Ed exclaimed, as if just realizing he had one of the greatest guards ever on his team. "Oscar! You're here! What—what are we gonna do now?"

I was too busy slapping my hand over my mouth to hear what Oscar said, but Oscar did offer a new strategy, and then we did it, and then even though my memory is a bit hazy on the details, I'm almost certain it worked.

Oscar's been forgotten among NBA fans, analysts, and media since his playing days. The consensus is he's one of the best 10 or 15 players ever (I'd put him No. 1, but that's my bias for you) and yet you don't hear his name nearly as much as Russell, Jordan, Magic, Bird, or even Barkley or Duncan. I have a theory about this, and I suspect I hold this theory because I empathize with it: Oscar doesn't really have a place he belongs in the history of basketball.

Oscar spent most of his career with Cincinnati, a city that doesn't have an NBA team anymore, and he spent the last part of his career with the Milwaukee Bucks, where he won a championship but played second fiddle to Kareem Abdul-Jabbar. After four seasons with the Bucks, Oscar retired. Some might say he belongs to Indiana, but I think Oscar would take issue with that concept and that phrasing. He experienced horrible racism during his high school and college career, and if his writing has been any indication, he doesn't want to associate with Indiana in the same way Indiana didn't want to associate with him while he was a player.

So, for all his successes, Oscar wasn't able to build a true basketball connection to any one place, and I think that hurts his legacy a lot. Los Angeles will always celebrate, promote, and welcome back Kareem and Magic and Jerry West, and Boston will do the same for Bird and Russell. Jordan will be associated with Chicago forever, same with Dr. J and Charles Barkley in Philadelphia. Heck, my brother Dick spent most of his career with the Phoenix Suns; he's now known as the "Original Sun" and his name and number are in the team's Ring of Honor. Cities love finding and embracing local heroes, but Oscar doesn't have a place to embrace him. His memory relies only on that—memory—and it's up to old teammates, coaches, and friends like me—to keep the stories of his greatness circulating.

I relate to Oscar's basketball homelessness. I was sort of a nomad in the NBA. I never played in one place long enough to establish myself within the team's broader community (this is professionally speaking—Indiana has always celebrated my amateur career). My best years in the pros were with the Royals, but they're gone, and I'm not really a part of Detroit, Philadelphia, Atlanta, or Phoenix. I can't say I regret this about my career—there's nothing I could've done different—but it's hard to consider both Oscar and me in this way. To receive an ovation from a city you gave so much to, that would be special. I wish I had that.

My dad, Dick, me, and my dog Pal

Jon McGlocklin, Dick, me, IU teammates, SAE Roommates,
and fellow NBA'ers

Dave DeBusschere my 1st NBA Coach

Detroit Pistons team 1966-67

Memorable Indiana friends Jimmy Rayl and Tom Bolyard, IU teammates; Ray Pavy in chair, Bill Shover with the tie, who mentored Dick and me through High School and NBA days, with his son Kevin.

Captain Tom Van Arsdale and Coach Bob Cousy

Me and Oscar Robertson

Hilda Van Arsdale at Bob & Karen Knight Wedding
(Pastor is on left)

My mom and wife Kathy 1977 NBA Retirement

My Womb Mate

But I will always admire how Oscar, despite his lack of NBA roots, gave so much of himself to the league. He was one of the best off-the-court advocates the pros have ever had. He fought restlessly for our rights as employees, public figures, and athletes, and he played a huge role in inspiring my own advocacy for NBA players.

Sportswriters and NBA historians know about the Oscar Robertson Rule, but I'd be surprised if some of the younger guys in the current league know why they earn such lucrative contracts and enjoy so many transactional freedoms. Modern player empowerment is rooted in a 1970 case between Oscar—then the head of the NBA Players Association—and the NBA. It was a class-action lawsuit, and it posed a number of anti-trust solutions to the way the NBA treated its players. Oscar fought the case before, during, and after his retirement, and a settlement finally came in 1976. His work gave pros a number of new benefits, including:

1. An end to the "option clause," which said players were bound to the team that drafted them for life, unless that team wanted to trade them. This was the first step toward unrestricted free agency in the NBA, which arrived in 1988.

2. Compensation for players who suffered damages (less lucrative contracts) under the old option clause. These guys received payouts between $1,900 and $29,000—a decent amount back then.

3. The ability for players, upon being drafted, to opt out of signing a contract. Guys could instead choose to sit out a year and re-enter the draft the next season.

4. Eligibility for all high school graduates to enter the NBA draft.

The lawsuit changed basketball forever, and if you ask me, everyone from Tom Chambers to LeBron James owes Oscar the sincerest thank you. Oscar never enjoyed the benefits he earned for his peers and successors, but the fight was worth it to him anyway. It was an incredible example to me of a way I could turn my basketball career into something that could impact the NBA beyond what I did in a game.

I had a front-row seat to much of Oscar's activism. When I served on the NBA Players Association, we'd fly to Manhattan during our free weekends and meet with our attorneys about the latest rounds of negotiations with the league (the NBA's lead attorney at the time was none other than future commissioner David Stern). These were intense conversations, but Oscar always asserted himself among the power-players, using his status as a superstar to gain leverage. He was tremendous in that respect. He wasn't verbose or chatty, but he was always direct, and he was completely convicted in his beliefs. He wouldn't kowtow to anybody. Instead, he sacrificed to help the rest of us along.

I was never a superstar, but Oscar's demeanor in those meetings made me better realize the role I could play as an advocate myself. I had expertise about business, and I certainly had opinions about what we deserved as players, but as I went forward from the Players Association to eventually the Retired Players Association, I learned how to be a supplement to the stars who could really throw around their influence. Those guys are sticking their neck out and using their platform, so that means guys like me can do the dirty work to make sure they're in a position to stay in good standing with all the suits. It takes teamwork and balance, everyone sacrificing, and it's special when you see superstars staking their reputations on to deals right next to role players.

Serving on the Retired Players Association with Oscar was great for our friendship. I think true friends connect over more than a few common interests; they share missions, too. At board meetings for the RPA, I'd be around the same table as Oscar, Dave Cowens, Dave Bing, Archie Clark, Maurice Lucas, Fred Brown, and Bob Petit—all of whom were All Stars, four of whom are Hall of Famers—but we all cut it up and talked shop as if our varying legacies were left outside. We were a diverse cross-section of the NBA, but we were united under a common purpose. That's how sports bring different kinds of people together. Their unifying power has nothing to do with putting a bunch of jocks in the same room, or putting a couple Hoosiers on the same team—it's about mission. Oscar and I retain our mutual values today, and that's why our friendship continues. We'll always be fighting for the same things.

Oscar is one of the most important people I have ever met, both in a broader sense and personal sense. Obviously, as "the Big O" he was a legend. He changed basketball and impacted every future generation of NBA players. But my relationship with him transcends the sport. To me, he's Oscar, the guy I'd prank with cigarettes on planes, the guy who picked up our restaurant and bar tabs out on the road before we could put up a fight, the guy who'd stay up with me arguing about the greatest players in the game, the guy who still starts every conversation we have with, "How's Dick?" Oscar gave me my ultimate confidence as a basketball player, and he lit a fire in me to become an advocate for my fellow athletes. He really changed my life. I can't believe someone I used to look up to so much became one of my closest friends, and I can't believe that the closer I became to him, I only found more reasons to admire him. Oscar is one of the most authentic, sensitive people I know. He's seen so much disrespect and mistreatment in his life that all apologies have vanished from his vocabulary. That makes him tough, sure, but it also makes him honest, loyal, and virtuous. He asked everyone to take him or leave him, and on the court or off, I don't hesitate to take him every time. Oscar Robertson is my friend. That has to be worth at least a couple playoff games.

Chapter Eight

I think a lot about a basketball player most people have never heard of named Raymond Lewis. In the late 1960s, Raymond Lewis was one of the best young guards in America. He was an early-generation streetballer, an undersized kid—about 6'1"—who could play above his size, mostly because he had a lot of ego and confidence. Raymond won three straight high school state championships in California, and as a sophomore at Cal State LA, he averaged 33 points per game, second in the entire nation. He had college games in which he scored over 50, 60, even 70 points. His resumé spoke for itself, and in 1973, the Philadelphia 76ers selected him 18th overall in the NBA draft. I was on the Sixers then. Raymond was going to be our savior.

I've explained the attitudes of NBA players in training camp already—it doesn't matter if Superman is trying to make the team, the veterans will do anything to keep the Man of Steel from taking their spot. Well, in this case Raymond Lewis was Superman, but that didn't matter. We had to protect our jobs.

I remember when Raymond arrived at camp. He had new shoes and a big gym bag, and his entitlement was practically lifting him off the ground. It was like he owned the place. Raymond tossed his towel on the ground and clapped for someone to feed him a pass and when the ball came, he did a couple showboat California moves and took it to the basket. He was flashy, alright. I noticed some of the guys giving Raymond harder stares than they usually would a rookie. That was a bad sign. Guys took note of his dribble, his release, all his little

121

hitches and hesitations and tendencies. They were putting together their personal scouting reports on Raymond Lewis. There was going to be a scrimmage that afternoon.

We set up our intra-squad game after lunch. Shootaround was tight—there was an edge to the atmosphere—and then we started play. It was ruthless. I don't remember many of the finer details of the scrimmage, but one thing is certain: Raymond Lewis never made a basket. I lost count of how many times guys stole his dribble or blocked his shot. When he brought the ball up, guys pressed him like a diner burger, and when he manned up on defense, guys screened him like a bug on the porch. It wasn't outright malicious, but it was a message in capital letters: If You Want to Be In the NBA, Earn It. The veterans embarrassed Raymond Lewis that day. His game looked terrible.

The next morning, we all woke up and headed in for another practice, but when we arrived, someone was missing: Raymond. Maybe he was having his ankles taped, or maybe he was still grabbing breakfast. Someone checked the trainer's office, but there was no Raymond. Someone else went to his room—no Raymond. In fact, Raymond's room was completely empty. We soon found out from a team official: Raymond had packed his bags and left.

I've heard other parties say Raymond left because of a contract dispute with the 76ers, or because our coach—Gene Shue—wanted him to sit out his rookie season and mature, but my take is Raymond left because he knew he couldn't make it in the pros. He probably didn't think we were better than he was or more talented, but he saw how hard we worked to keep our jobs, and he just didn't want to make the same kind of effort. That group of 76ers, as you'll see later on, wasn't exactly a loaded roster of Hall of Famers. We were a simple crew of NBA workmen, pure and ego-less professionals. If Raymond couldn't hang with us, he wasn't going to be able to hang with anybody. He knew it, and we knew it. To be honest, I always kind of felt sorry for Raymond. He missed out by quitting.

I tell this story as a way to introduce my time with the Cincinnati Royals, what some would consider the prime of my career. These were my age 24 to age 28 seasons, when I hit my physical peak, became one of the game's more well-regarded two-way players, and even picked up some honors for my efforts. Being in your prime is a hell of a lot of fun, but I preface it with the Raymond Lewis story to remind myself this: It was no guarantee.

***

Before we dive into my time as a Royal, I have to ask for a little grace so I can puff myself up a little. This book has mentioned and will mention a lot of disappoints about my NBA career, so here, I would humbly ask you to allow me an opportunity to pat myself on the back. I have to say: I had a pretty dang good run in Cincinnati.

The year I was traded from the Pistons to the Royals, I averaged fewer than 8 points per game at a shooting rate below 40 percent. Not great. But my first full year in Cincinnati, under my new coach Ed Jucker and alongside Oscar Robertson in the backcourt, I leapt up to 19 points per game on 44 percent shooting, with almost 7 free throw attempts per game as reward for my aggressiveness. The next three seasons were doubtless my best: I made the NBA All Star team three straight times, from 1970 to 1972, and averaged over 20 points per game across that stretch. In 1970, I was a top-10 scorer in all of basketball—ninth in the league in total points and 10th in scoring average, with 23 points per game on 45 percent shooting. I was really a somebody—that's pretty good!

Success is born of opportunity, they say, and I think opportunity comes from hard work. After my arrival in Cincinnati, I began to commit myself further to my development as a player. I had a little seasoning at that point—I was used to the strength and speed of the pros by then—but it was time to adapt my skillset in response to my new savviness.

The first step was harnessing my take-no-shit attitude on the court. Years of honing my competitive spirit against Dick in Greenwood paid off in Cincinnati, where I turned everything into a chance to prove myself. I hurtled through picks, took charges, and transformed my aggressive drives to the basket into high-flying attacks on the defense. I turned everything into a competition. I gassed myself in drills, tracked my personal records and tried to beat them, and took every comment from Coach Jucker or Oscar or any other veteran to heart. Heck, I was so eager to improve I remember trying to win the end-of-practice wind sprints. I was a real son of a bitch—or as us old-timers say: I didn't have any candy-ass in me.

At the end of training camp before my first full season with the Royals, Coach Jucker announced I had made the starting lineup. I was thrilled, but a little surprised. I was replacing Adrian Smith, a former All-Star game MVP and an eight-year veteran in Cincinnati. He was a tough guy to muscle out of the rotation. But Jucker expressed confidence in my game. He took to my style of play, and what's more, he thought I was the best fit next to Oscar. It was the ignition I needed to become a top-notch player.

Being a starter empowered me to take that statistical leap I explained earlier, but the better numbers were more than a product of greater minutes. By this point, it was my fourth season in the league, I was just a more skilled player, and the Royals' offense was partially designed to take advantage of my specific skills. As the shooting guard next to Oscar, I had lots of room to move off the ball. I could run off picks, initiate sets, call for a shot, slice to the basket—a whole permutation of moves. I was stronger and faster than I had been in Detroit, too, and that meant I could finish harder through contact, put more lift on my jump shot, and. hang longer in the air. On defense, I could bust through more screens, shuffle faster to stay in front of my man, and be quicker to contest shots and gamble for steals. I was at a point where only the game's superstars—Oscar, Russell, Wilt—had a noticeable athletic advantage on me.

That physical growth partnered with some fresh maturity, too. I put in extra work in Cincinnati, making two fundamental changes to my game that opened up my scoring ability. First, I changed the timing on my jump shot to quicken my release, letting the ball go on my way up rather than at the peak of my jump. If you're familiar with shooting mechanics, you'll know this release point makes the shot tougher to block—defenders have to react faster—and adds a little more range. Shooting on the way up gathers more momentum from your legs behind the ball, and that lets you shoot farther. When you don't have to muscle shots toward the rim, your mechanics stay consistent, and for me, that meant more buckets.

I added a pump fake to my repertoire, too. Bob Cousy, my second coach in Cincinnati, took to my fast-paced style of play even more than Jucker did (Cousy was a pioneer of the fast break offense as the primary ball handler on the famous Celtics teams of the 1960s). He wanted to give me more options during my attack, so he taught me a move that had me fake a drive before stopping short of the hoop and juking my head and shoulders to bait my defender into going for a chase-down block against the backboard. As soon as my defender bit on the fake and jumped into the air, I'd go up toward the hoop, draw their contact, and have a three-point play. Those were some of the easiest baskets of my career, and when more timid defenders went soft against me to avoid being fooled, well, that just made it easier for me to go hard to the basket without a fake. Cousy's coaching made me a more unpredictable offensive player.

Hitting your prime comes with experience, and almost every pro has to put in repetitions before they have a complete feel for the game. Some guys flourish right away—Oscar averaged 30/10/9 as a rookie, and LeBron James averaged 20/5/5—but most guys have to grow into the pros. Kobe Bryant and Steph Curry had to grind for a few years before they blossomed, same with Steve Nash and Dirk Nowitzki. You have to build confidence in yourself, the kind of confidence that makes you feel comfortable with your shortcomings and open to improvement: *I want to compete, I want to work hard, I want to prove I belong in the NBA.*

I never thought it was a guarantee that I'd reach my prime, and that's probably why I reached it in the first place.

***

My best basketball years coincided with my best teams as well, but unfortunately, that wasn't a high bar to hit in my career. In the 1968-69 season, we went 41-41 in Cincinnati, which is the best record any of my teams ever achieved (we still missed the playoffs by a rather startling 7 whole games—the Celtics, right above us in the standings, went 48-34 and actually won the championship). At the time, it was only a mild disappointment to miss those playoffs because, by and large, our team had been competitive throughout the season, but perhaps if I had known then how the rest of my career would turn out, I would've been a little more dissatisfied.

But no matter how optimistic I felt about the Royals' future prospects, team management felt different: Ed Jucker was fired after the 1968-69 season, and in his place the Royals brought in Hall of Fame point guard Bob Cousy. It was Cousy's first coaching gig in the pros (he had retired as a player in 1963), and while the switch could have spelled doom for my development, I was fortunate that Cousy saw all the same strengths in me as my old coach.

But not only did Cousy recognize my talent and work ethic, he wanted to take even greater advantage of my strengths than Jucker did. As I grew into my prime, Coach Cousy began to shape the Cincinnati offense around my skillset, drawing up schemes and plays specifically to give me the ball with an opportunity to score. A perfect example: the first time I scored over 40 points. Give me a moment to put on my proverbial letterman jacket, because it's time for me to be the washed-up jock talking about his glory days.

I remember the game well (seriously, indulge me here—I just said my best season only had 41 wins, for crying out loud). We were playing the mighty Los Angeles Lakers at the Forum in Los Angeles, with Jerry West, Wilt Chamberlain, and Elgin Baylor on the other end of the floor. Cousy had installed a system that would free me up for some shots. In his design, the center would move to one side of the basket while the two forwards—myself and Jerry Lucas— would set up in the other lane. I'd position myself down by the basket while Lucas carved out his territory closer to the free throw line. During a typical play, Lucas would set a screen on my man and I'd run around him to catch the ball near the top of the key. From there, I could take an open jump shot if Lucas had impeded my defender, or I could put my defender on my hip and drive past him if he had fought through Jerry's screen (good luck with that—Jerry was so strong I once saw him punch straight through a door). Either way, I had a quality shot.

L.A. had a great team in 1969. They deployed one of the best defenses in the league (second overall that year by defensive rating) behind that trio of offensive superstars. At the end of the season, they ended up in the Finals, but you wouldn't have guessed that on November 2, though. That night, I pasted them.

Elgin Baylor was guarding me, thank goodness. He's one of the great scorers the NBA has ever known, but on defense...let's just say he wasn't the most caring defender. During the game, whenever Jerry set that screen for me, Elgin almost never had the motivation to fight through it. That meant I was open a lot, and that meant I had a lot of opportunities to either shoot or drive. The opposing defense could take away that decision and force me to pass if the interior defender moved out from under the basket to challenge my shot, but that night, Wilt Chamberlain just never came out. I had open 15-footers all night. And I just couldn't miss.

My highlight reel from the game would look like a broken instant replay machine—just the same straightaway midrange jumper over and over. Swish. Swish. Swish. It was so repetitious I remember thinking as the ball left my hands: *What the heck is going on here? Why won't anyone cover me? Why do I have so much time to even ask these questions during a game?* It was automatic. I ended the game with 41 points, and for all the energy Elgin saved playing defense against me, I held him to just 15 points of his own, on 4 of 17 shooting, at the other end. I had a dominant, complete two-way game. Everything went right.

At least, that's how it felt in my book. After the game, I was celebrating with my teammates in the locker room when Coach Cousy approached, his expression neutral. I grinned at him. "Good game, Coach."

"Thank you, Tom. Next time you're coming off Jerry's screens, make sure you're real tight against his hip. Your spacing was a little loose in the second half."

I think I was silent for a good three seconds before I closed my gaping mouth and nodded. "You bet, Coach. I'll play it tight."

"Alright." And Bob Cousy left to review his notes from the game.

That was Cousy though, all the time. He was a perfectionist, another Oscar-type genius who's so keen on the game that the particulars sometimes obscured the bigger picture (this might be why Cousy and Oscar never had a strong relationship, come to think of it—in any case, their bickering resulted in Cousy trading Oscar to Milwaukee in 1970). Cousy cared as much about how you did something as he did the end result, and man, did he care about the end result.

As a personality, Cousy could be a bit of a loner and very shy, but underneath, he housed one of the most explosive tempers I have ever seen. He was a screamer and a yeller, but beyond that, his frustration would sometimes move him to tears. He always thought he could coach a team above their potential—something difficult, if not impossible, to do in the NBA, where talent does more to determine a team's ceiling than in probably any other sport. When Cousy felt like he was failing to elevate a roster through his leadership, he'd take it hard. Our Royals teams presented a lot of challenges to him in this manner.

I remember one halftime speech during his tenure in particular. Our performance in the game must have been pretty disappointing, because Cousy came into the locker room good and ready to lay into us. Sure enough, no sooner had the door slammed behind him that Cousy started yelling, and as he huffed and puffed about our slow rotations on defense and lazy cuts on offense, he actually began to heat up. It was like watching a starchy pot of pasta boiling over on the stove. Cousy was red in the face and foamy at the mouth and condensation beaded on his forehead. His eyes welled, and the waterworks began, tears welling from Cousy's eyes and rolling down his cheeks. And all the while he continued raging on about our lack of effort. It looked like he was downright losing his mind.

And sitting there with all the players, it was a *fascinating* performance. None of us had ever seen anything like it from a coach. Connie Dierking caught my eye and gave me the tiniest

Can you believe this shit? head shake, and Tiny Archibald, a rookie that season, kept swiveling his eyes between Cousy and the team as if he wasn't sure who to take more seriously. Norm Van Lier—who actually was dating Cousy's daughter at the time—looked terrified, naturally.

Cousy must have sensed he was losing the room, because somehow, inexplicably, impossibly, he entered another gear. He started moving around, pacing, gesticulating wildly with his arms like a frenzied traffic cop. *This must be the kind of passion that fueled him to all those championships*, I thought, watching spit fly from his lips onto Tiny Archibald's head. *I can't imagine how he'd react if this was a playoff game instead of a regular-season game. Would he have an aneurism? Who would coach if that happened? Could I coach?*

Meanwhile, some of the guys were starting to lose it. Connie Dierking couldn't suppress his laugh, but he disguised it with a strange, forced cough and moved his eyes to the floor. Fred Foster clapped both hands over his mouth. I took some deep breaths. If Cousy saw us laughing, the Cincinnati Police Department would have 12 fresh murder investigations on their hands.

NBA locker rooms back then were set up with little pharmaceutical stations, basically tables stocked with vitamins, supplements, and other substances for the players to take at their discretion (I know that sounds suspicious, but trust me, these stations were mostly vitamin C and salt tablets, maybe some aspirins, nothing illegal). In Cincinnati, our vitamin table was up toward the front—in this case, right next to Cousy.

It was inevitable. Cousy's up there swinging his arms around like a lunatic. Everybody's frozen, watching him. The table's right there. And it happens. Cousy swings his right arm wide and high, his hips turn, his voice cracks like a bullwhip, and then, like a juiced-up baseball player taking a swing for the fences, he whips his arm back down and across his body and abso-fucking-lutely *annihilates* the vitamin table. Pills go flying into the air like buckshot, bottles careen off the walls, tablets scatter across the floor. All the players duck for cover, holding their arms over their heads and hunching down and turning away from the blast zone.

The clattering stops. Silence. I peek through my fingers. Connie Dierking lifts his head. Bob Cousy stands at the front of the room, panting. There's a small moment where all the players just look at one another. Then Cousy says:

"See everyone out there for the second half." And he leaves, the door shuts, and finally, we break, laughing and hooting and pegging one another with vitamins. I don't remember how we did in the second half. It doesn't really matter.

***

Given all that, I never was offended or taken down by a coach—seriously! Even Cousy's tantrums just made me want to go out and work harder. I was already tough on myself, so while I'd always be affirmed when a coach like Cousy had a good word for me, I never took criticism personally. It just bounced right off.

My second season under Cousy, the first Royals season after Oscar left, Cousy approached me in training camp and said I had been made team captain. That was a nice honor. It doesn't really affect your role on the team—there's no special privileges or responsibilities—but it comes with the expectation that you're the guy in the locker room who keeps the team focused, motivated, and encouraged. You're a spokesman for the guys, and you can be a liaison of sorts between them and the coach. In other words, it's your job as a captain to have a good relationship with everyone. That was easy for me.

One thing Cousy and I unexpectedly aligned on was race. He was teammates with Bill Russell during his years on the Celtics, and while that made Cousy very aware of racial injustice, he's faced criticism in his old age for not doing enough to elevate and advocate for his black peers as one of the league's premiere white superstars in the 50s and 60s. Cousy's expressed a lot of regret about that, but I will say that as the Royals' coach, he was actually very thoughtful about race relations.

During one practice—I'm not sure how this happened, because the Royals didn't have many explicit issues with race that I can remember—Cousy noticed that all the white players were shooting on one hoop and all the black players were shooting on a different hoop. There was no hostility or prejudice going on, but it was a divided gym, so Cousy approached me as the captain and said, "Hey Tom, could you get the guys to mingle a little bit more?"

Cousy didn't know about my history with the public basketball courts in Indiana, so he had unwittingly approached someone on the team who had experience with this very thing. I saw what he meant right away. "Sure thing, Coach." I grabbed some guys and brought them with me to the other basket, and that was it. There wasn't anything formal about the move; our team was full of strong relationships between all kinds of players, so we integrated easily and fell right back into shootaround. Looking back, I admire how Cousy wasn't complacent on the issue. He pursued inclusivity with intention, and he kept a high standard. That was the strong side of his perfectionism.

***

The other exciting honor I received during my time in Cincinnati: All Star. I was a three-time All Star in my NBA career. Today, fans have 50 percent of the voting power for the All-Star rosters, but when I played, a panel of sportswriters and broadcasters picked the top eight players in each conference before the league's coaches filled out the rest of the teams through their own vote. I was one of the players chosen by the coaches for my first All Star selection in 1970. Another perk of all that hustle, I guess!

The All-Star game now has a lot of pageantry and flash, but in my day it had a more prestigious tone. I was just one of 24 players across the whole league to be named an All-Star and given the concentration of talent in the league back then, my company in the Eastern Conference (then the Eastern Division) was almost appallingly elite. I looked around the locker room before the game in 1970 and saw no less than nine Hall of Famers, including Kareem Abdul-Jabbar, Walt Frazier, John Havlicek, and Willis Reed. *My God*, I thought, *I'm on a team with these guys?* It was just plain awesome, and it made me feel really proud.

People always want to know if the All-Star game has a secret level of competition to it, if the players really want to beat each other and put up big numbers. It's not true, and I think the question actually comes from a misconception about the league as a whole.

First, the All-Star game itself is not very serious, but the players do want to look good. The idea is you go out, play with pride, put on a show for the fans, but never do anything to hurt or hammer another player. This wasn't where you nursed a grudge or doled out a grievance. It was show time. Sure, every time a bunch of athletes come together, there's going to be some competition, but there was never anything mean-spirited at All-Star Weekend. It was in the pure spirit of basketball—we just had fun.

Second, I think fans see the All-Star game as a rare chance for the top end of the league's talent pool to come together and interact, because that's one of the few times the fans see that group together on TV. In actuality, the gathering isn't that unusual. We players would see each other all the time on the road, going out to dinner together, visiting each other's homes, catching up before and after games. My first year as an All Star, I had Dave DeBusschere with me on the Eastern team. Jimmy Walker was there, too, and so was Oscar. Practicing with those guys again and hanging with them in the locker room felt like a big reunion. We'd be paraded around all weekend to dinners and other functions, and that was fun because it gave us the chance to goof around together. Fans see the All-Star game as a talent showcase, but I really see it as a showcase for the camaraderie of the NBA.

135

Oh, and I had a pretty good relationship with one of the guys on the Western Division team in 1970: Dick Van Arsdale. My brother and I were All Stars on opposing teams for two different seasons. The second time we both made it—1971—he asked me if I wanted to swap jerseys and switch teams for the game! I was a fun-sucker and I said no, but it was more because I didn't want to make a farce of the event than because I was scared to be caught. If Oscar or Jerry Lucas or any of our other close pals had sniffed us out, I'm sure they just would've thought it was funny.

***

Looking at my NBA resumé on paper, it might surprise some people to see how many Hall of Famers I had relationships with—if I was never on a playoff team, how did I manage to connect with people like Oscar, Jerry West, Sam Jones, and Bill Bradley? Or Jerry Lucas, John Havlicek, Billy Cunningham, Dave Bing, and Gail Goodrich? The names are kind of unbelievable all in a row, and that's a testament to how enmeshed and distinguished the NBA experience is. Those guys are my brothers in arms, family members, close friends, and fellow native speakers in the land of basketball. They understand one of the most important things in my life, and I understand that central part of them, too.

But Jerry Lucas is another story.

Well, Jerry Lucas is actually more like three other stories.

Hall of Famer, NBA champion, Rookie of the Year, 7-time All Star, 5-time All-NBA honoree, career averages of 17 points and 15 rebounds per game. That's Jerry Lucas on paper, at least in basketball terms. Outside of basketball, Jerry was much more complicated—an aspiring fast food mogul, close-up magician, toy entrepreneur, and memory whiz. He would go on Johnny Carson and meet everyone in the audience and an hour later recite every single one of their names. He wrote 30 books on memory and learning, and he devoted most of his post-NBA career to children's education, even hosting a TV special in the 1970s called "The Jerry Lucas Super Kids Day Magic Jamboree" (let me know if you want an editor for future brand ideas, Jerry).

All that's to say: Jerry Lucas is one of my closest relationships from basketball, but he's also one of the flat-out weirdest people I've met in my life.

First off, Jerry was probably a genius (and geniuses are usually pretty weird!). I remember during our time together on the Royals—we teamed up for the better part of two seasons in Cincinnati—we would carpool to the airport before road trips. On one drive, Jerry's at the wheel and he asks me, "Hey Tom, do you know how many of those dotted dividing lines there are in a mile on the highway?"

I was surprised by the question. I raised an eyebrow. "No Jerry...do you?"

Jerry Lucas nodded. "Mhmm. 264."

I was stunned. Had he counted them?

Another time, we were in the lobby of an ad agency in New York City, waiting for someone to come meet us about a promo for Jerry's entrepreneurial fast food endeavor, Jerry Lucas Beef 'N Shakes. The ceiling was made out of those acoustic tiles, the kind with all the holes in them. I noticed Jerry studying the tiles.

"Hey Tom." Uh oh.

I sighed. "Yeah Jerry?"

Jerry Lucas pointed. "You know how many holes are in each of those ceiling tiles?"

"No."

Silence.

I looked at Jerry. He was just looking at the ceiling. I glanced up and then looked back to Jerry. He was going to sit there until I asked him. I opened my mouth. "...Do you, Jerry?"

Jerry Lucas nodded. "Mhmm. 7,112."

I looked back up at the tiles. There were a lot of holes. I didn't feel like checking his math. "Huh. Thanks Jerry."

"Sure thing, Tom."

Jerry Lucas Beef 'N Shakes was a saga unto itself. In the late 1960s, Jerry started a chain of restaurants in Ohio under the name—you guessed it—Jerry Lucas Beef 'N Shakes (they sold beef sandwiches and milkshakes—Jerry had a way with names, you see). Around the time I came aboard the Royals, Jerry was looking to expand his empire of meat and dairy into Indiana, and he asked Dick and me to partner with him. I'll be honest: Coming from Jerry Lucas, that proposition made me feel like the king of the world. Here was one of the most famous athletes in the United States, one of the game's great players, asking me and my brother to go into business with him. That was exciting. That's the great thing about being friends with someone like

Jerry, who's so passionate across so many interests: it's contagious. Both Dick and I said yes right away.

Now, I had an economics degree from Indiana University, but that didn't prepare me for the ordeal of Jerry Lucas Beef 'N Shakes. Overnight after my agreement, I was thrown into conversations about leasing buildings, borrowing money, marketing, and accounting that I had no business being involved with, and that was before all the talk about food preparation, cleanliness, health codes, and menu pricing. I was way, way over my head.

To make matters more intimidating, Jerry was an extremely hands-on, do-it-yourself businessperson. He was capable of a lot of things, but when it came to Beef 'N Shakes, his refusal to lean on any outside help hurt him a lot. Jerry purchased a plastic extruding machine to make all the signage himself, but he wanted to design all the packaging, and set all the prices, and sketch out the blueprints for every location's interior. He never brought in any consultation or outside input, and that meant in all the places Dick and I needed help, we were at a total loss. The person we were supposed to refer to was Jerry himself.

Well, Jerry Lucas Beef 'N Shakes proved unsustainable. Dick and I tried to open a couple locations in Indiana, but they both tanked and we lost a fair bit of money. It was a valuable experience for me, but it was a scared-straight experience. From then on, I vowed to be in greater control of my off-court ventures. I've been a lot savvier about that since then.

Jerry Lucas Beef 'N Shakes went bankrupt in 1969. Its failure has fallen in line with an unfortunate pattern in Jerry's business life, and I know that pattern has hurt a lot of his basketball relationships. For me, though, I was still happy to be friends with Jerry after the whole fiasco. He didn't intentionally try to hurt me or my brother, and besides, at the time we were barely 25, and almost embarrassingly naïve. It was a good learning experience.

Jerry Lucas embodies the benefit I felt of playing in a league that attracted personnel from all walks of life. There's a lot of perspective to be gleaned as an NBA player, but what's most instructive for me is looking at how each of my peer's backgrounds and upbringings impacted the way they handle the profession of being a famous basketball player. I had brilliant, Ivy-League teammates who didn't have the faintest concept of money, and I had teammates raised in dysfunctional, unstable neighborhoods who matured into some of the most successful businessmen I know. I saw privileged guys go broke, and disadvantaged guys become incredibly wealthy. Dick and I thought we had a chance with Jerry Lucas Beef 'N Shakes, but we were wrong, and we didn't execute properly. That's really it. I don't blame the old me for falling in with Jerry. He was the kind of guy who seemed to attract bizarre-o experiences.

***

My favorite story from my time on the Royals has absolutely nothing to do with basketball, except it happened to take place during one of our favorite road trips of the season: San Francisco.

I loved going to San Francisco to play the Warriors. We'd stay at the now-infamous Jack Tar Hotel on Van Ness

Boulevard—it was demolished in 2013, but back in those days it boasted closed-circuit television and a rooftop ice-skating rink—and rent a car to cruise around the night before the game. We'd usually go to Sausalito to sit on the pier and have dinner and drinks, then go to bed late and wake up the next to play the Warriors (it occurs to me now this routine probably gave San Francisco a distinct competitive advantage).

One time during a SF trip, Nate Thurmond, the Hall of Fame center for the Warriors, invited us out to his bar downtown. Nate was the greatest. He was footloose and fancy free and a total sweetheart, a walking guarantee to have a fun night. A group of us—me, Connie, and Jerry Lucas—accepted his invitation and headed over for dinner.

It was a typically rowdy night for a few twenty-somethings with extra money—a lot of good food and an inadvisable number of drinks—but as we were wrapping up the meal, one of Nate's buddies came into the place. Right away, you knew this guy was a character. He wore dark glasses he wouldn't take off and a cocked fedora on his head. Every now and then he'd pinch the brim of the fedora and run his hand along the edge like he was sealing an envelope. His movements were smooth as bourbon. You just liked watching him.

Oh, and in one hand this fellow also held a little dog on the end of a leash. That was a little unusual.

Nate saw his buddy walk in and he stood right up. "My man! How you doing, brother?" The two of them clasped hands and embraced. Nate gestured toward all of us. "We have some Royals in the house tonight."

"Ooh-wee! Royals!" The man with the dog flashed a big smile—was that a gold tooth? —and shook all our hands. "Pleasure to meet you, boys. You enjoying the recreation time?"

We all said we were. Connie Dierking pointed to the pooch. "What kind of dog is that?" he asked. The dog was a little old thing. Skinny legs, pointy ears, white wiry hair. It had a strange manner, kind of skittish and twitchy, the total opposite of its handler.

"Oh, this cat here?" the man said, gesturing— ironically—to his dog. "This is Mr. Ladies' Man."

Mr. Ladies' Man??

Connie and I laughed, but Jerry seemed intrigued. "Does Mr. Ladies' Man know any tricks?"

The man raised his eyebrows above his glasses for a moment. He gave a great guffaw and clapped his hands and did a little wiggling dance, like he was the host of a game show telling us to *Come on down!* "Oh, I'm glad you asked, fella. Mr. Ladies' Man knows the greatest trick of them all! Come and see!" And just like that he pivoted on his heel and struck on out for the front door.

Jerry, Connie, and I looked at each other, baffled. Nate grinned. "You guys better see this." We all followed the man outside.

We grouped up on the sidewalk and the man reached down and unclipped the leash from Mr. Ladies' Man. The dog sat hunched over, quivering. It looked up at all of us with big, wet eyes. It was really kinda cute. "Now watch this, fellas," said the owner, and he snapped his fingers at Mr. Ladies' Man: "Okay Mr. Ladies' Man, do your trick! Do your trick!"

And little Mr. Ladies' Man lifted up both his hind legs and began doing a walking handstand down the sidewalk. Just walking on its front paws.

"No way," I said aloud.

"Holy shit," said Connie.

"I could do that," said Jerry Lucas.

The owner clapped his hands and waved them over his dog like he was center ring at the circus. "Not bad, right boys? Not bad!" Nate stood by, chuckling.

But then Mr. Ladies' Man started to wobble. He did a little U-turn on the pavement and started heading back toward us, still only on its two front feet. He trembled. He looked strained. And then...he just started taking a piss.

Agh! We all leaped out of the way. It was a wild piss, the kind of spray that must only come out when Mr. Ladies' Man can't hold it anymore no matter how hard he tries. It went *everywhere*—the sidewalk, the street, the owner's shiny fresh trousers—like a fire hydrant on a summer day or a garden hose with the power on too high. Mr. Ladies' Man kept pissing and walking and pissing and walking and trying so hard to be a good boy, but oh man, he just couldn't help himself. His eyes were round and huge and when it was all over, he looked up at his owner with what can only be described as the sincerest form of humiliation.

At that point, I lose track of the story, because all I can remember is that Connie and Jerry and I were laughing so hard we could barely see, hear, or speak. We howled. We doubled over. Connie had to sit down he couldn't handle it. I'm not sure I've laughed harder in my life. When we finally pulled it together, Mr. Ladies' Man was back on the leash. His owner frowned behind his glasses. "That was not very cool, Mr. Ladies' Man. Not very cool at all."

But the ever-slick Nate Thurmond stepped in to save the day. He clapped his buddy on the back. "Hey hey, Mr. Ladies' Man always knows how to give the people what they want." He then shook our hands goodbye, grinning. "Another memorable night in the Bay, fellas. See you boys tomorrow."

We laughed the whole way home. I remember that night out more clearly than I remember most of my basketball games.

***

For most of my basketball life, I had struggled to feel like I truly belonged. I always had to prove to myself I had what it took to compete with the Crispus Attucks High Schools and the Michigans and the Boston Celtics—it never seemed right that a pointy-elbowed kid from Greenwood could go toe-to-toe with athletes who ought to have been, and often were, my childhood heroes. That finally changed for me in Cincinnati.

With the Royals, I played with my idol. Oscar gave me a confidence that told me how much I could contribute to a team. Beyond him, I played for coaches—Ed Jucker and Bob Cousy—who never saw a need to corral my style of play. Rather, they embraced it and treated it like an asset. And I played with teammates—Oscar, Jerry, Connie, Adrian Smith, Fred Foster, Nate Williams, Sam Lacey, Butch Fehr, Norm Van Lier, Tiny Archibald, Pat Frink—who accepted me as a friend. We went out together and shared meals together and pulled pranks on each other and learned the ins and outs of each other's lives. We were a fraternity. I admired them, and I was one of them.

Cincinnati itself reminded me a little bit of home. It had a charm to it, a hospitality, an easy friendliness that made you feel like you knew someone on every block. Sort of like Greenwood. I bought a house there, and a membership to the country club, and sometimes I imagined myself spending many years there. Of course, that wasn't meant to be—the Royals moved to Kansas City after the 1972 season (changing their name to the Kings along the way), and I was traded in early 1973 to the Philadelphia 76ers. It takes some luck to build a legacy in one place.

Sportswriters talk about a player's prime in athletic terms, but it should be more than that. You're lucky to enjoy your prime in an environment where the basketball feels like a bonus, where you can place the game within a broader context of community, freedom, and personal growth and see yourself mature in ways that go beyond the court. I had that in Cincinnati. Not every player can say their best years on the floor were also their most fun, but I can. That's fortunate. I had tough years behind me in Detroit, and even tougher years ahead of me in Philly and Atlanta, but I spent my prime in Cincinnati, where I flourished into the best version of my basketball self and a better version of my personal self.

My time on the Royals was 50 years ago now. That's hard to wrap my head around. Life goes by fast. As I grow older, my NBA career concentrates more and more in my memory, but as it does, the recollections that remain become a purer representation of everything that was most important to me about basketball. When I read the old game logs from my seasons in Cincinnati, I find numerous things I've forgotten. I had a game-winning buzzer beater against my brother Dick and the Phoenix Suns in 1969. I had multiple 40-point games, a streak of three straight games over 30 points, and 12 straight games over 20 points (with a 44-point effort in there for good measure—how about that!). But the games and statistics don't stick with me. I just remember the car rides to the airport with Jerry Lucas, the nights in San Francisco with my friends and Nate Thurmond, and the little talks at practice with Coach Cousy. Those memories are the ones that stay with me the most. It's funny how that works. After 12 years in the league, the thing about the NBA I think about the least, actually, is basketball.

Chapter Nine

I might never have left Cincinnati, but as with most of my major career moves, it was out of my control. After the 1971 season (my fourth full year with the team—we finished 30-52, six games out of the playoffs), the Royals' owners announced they were moving the team from Cincinnati to Kansas City, renaming us the Kings in the process (they didn't want us to be confused with the Kansas City Royals baseball team). It was a volatile and destabilizing period, and it was frustrating to have such a major transition dictated by other people's financial interests. I was cut off from the best local community I had found at that point in the NBA.

On top of that disruption, the move meant the team would split home games between the 7,000-seat Municipal Auditorium in Kansas City and—inexplicably—the 9,000-seat Omaha Civic Auditorium in Nebraska. That was a miserable schedule. We were essentially playing 61 road games a year. All the travel meant it was hard to feel rooted. I actually began hoping for a trade.

To make my immediate situation worse, Coach Cousy started giving away my PT during the 1972 season. I had suffered a mild but scary-looking spinal injury in 1971, and ever since, Cousy seemed to think I wasn't the same player. He'd stick me on the bench with the excuse that my injury had dulled my aggression. It was another place my agency was stifled.

And personally, I felt I could still contribute. Since that season, I've looked back on my statistics to see if there was a difference after my injury, and I'm proud to say there wasn't a significant drop-off. In 1971, before my injury, I averaged 24 points for every 36 minutes I played (per-36 numbers are a better indication of efficiency than per-game numbers), and over the course of that whole season, I averaged 19 points per 36 minutes. After my injury, I had games of 35, 31, 39, and 44 points, and if you look at my free throw attempts—a reliable sign of aggressiveness—I was only down half a free throw per game from my pre-injury average.

I hadn't lost much of my game at all, but apparently Cousy disagreed, so as the restrictions on my PT continued, I became antsy for a change. I just wanted a chance to keep contributing while I still had the ability. The worst thing you can do to a pro is take their playing time when they still have skill. We athletes are ticking physical clocks—we only have so long when we can be at our best.

But I didn't just cross my arms and pout. I had actually built myself a sort of escape route out of Kansas City—to Phoenix, Arizona, of all places. My brother Dick was putting together a fine career with the Suns, and I always had fun visiting him on the road and during holidays (you could walk around Phoenix on Christmas Eve in nothing but shorts and a t-shirt!), so during the summer of 1972, I made some moves to make myself a landing spot in Arizona. I bought a house in Phoenix, married a beautiful, smart, local girl named Kathy, and scouted out some real-estate opportunities Dick and I thought we could build a business upon once we retired. My hope was to be traded to the Suns, play with Dick, retire at the same time as him, and keep working together after the NBA. It was perfect. My heart was dead set on the desert. I honestly couldn't wait.

***

Maybe Bob Cousy could see my anticipation for a new situation when he approached me after practice during that 1972 season. "Tom, I'd like to talk to you."

I had been sitting on the sidelines for most of the afternoon—Cousy's orders. (It always felt a little strange resting while everyone else was practicing, which makes me wonder how guys can "load manage" today, but best to not work me up about that again.) I stood up. I could sense this was it. The writing was on the wall, and now the prophecy would be fulfilled. I was on the move.

"How are you, Coach?" I asked, trying to play it casual.

Cousy wasn't a time waster. "Fine. I've traded you."

Valley of the Sun, here I come. I knew I was supposed to be gracious and team-first, but I went off-script almost right away. "Cous, that's great"—whoops— "am I going to Phoenix?"

Cousy frowned. Thick lines creased on his forehead. "Phoenix? No. You're going to Philadelphia."

Oh. My. Gosh.

I was in complete shock. *Philadelphia? That Philadelphia? Not—no.* This wasn't the plan. How do I put this delicately— the 76ers that year were a clusterfuck.

If the 1972-73 Philadelphia 76ers were a car at a dealership, they'd be the burnt, faded, broken-down used lemon in the corner with the sticker price so low it was almost offensive: 4-47, the team's win-loss record at the time. Philadelphia had started the season with a 15-game losing streak, then had a 14-gamer in December and January, and at the precise moment of my trade had lost another nine in a row (this would stretch to an I-shit-you-not NBA record 21 straight losses). It was far from the land of saguaro and sunshine I had been hoping for, and I had no choice but to go. Can you imagine how a modern All Star would react to this kind of situation? If they had no free agency, no player empowerment, no choice? Hearing that news, I felt the limitations of my autonomy more than any other point in my career. I feel it now! Heck, I'm a little steamed just telling the story again!

But as Cousy left me agape on the practice floor, I remembered George Allen. Was there a positive opportunity on the other side of this change? I remembered my mom's attitude. Where was the clover in this field of shit? I mustered up all my optimism. I thought: *I'm still a good player. I can still score with the best of them. I might be able to help Philly win some games.* And so, I packed my bags and headed to the airport, and that was the end of my time as a Royal. I felt like anything but.

And oh boy, I'll say this, too: If I knew the full extent of what I was walking into, I might have jumped out of the plane the minute we had reached full altitude.

***

Bad teams are sometimes described as "dumpster fires." The 1972-73 Philadelphia 76ers were like if you put that flaming dumpster on wheels and sent it careening into the Macy's Thanksgiving Day parade. They were so awful you weren't sure whether to call it a spectacle, or carnage.

At the beginning of the 1972 season, the 76ers had hired a new coach named Roy Rubin. I never met him—thank goodness—but Freddie Carter, the team's leading scorer in 1972, told me Rubin was so inept there would have been little difference between him coaching the team and that gorilla in San Francisco who knew sign language.

Rubin was utterly out of his depth. He had no experience coaching in the NBA, and I'd venture to say he had no place coaching in the NBA. His resumé prior to the Sixers included 10 years of high-school coaching and 11 years of coaching at Long Island University-Brooklyn, a Division II program. Nevertheless, the Sixers signed him to a three-year, $300,000 deal fully guaranteed. That would be about $12 million per year in today's NBA, more than any coach in the league.

Freddie says Rubin was borderline delusional about the team. After the Sixers won a few exhibition games, the meaningless preseason contests in which the good teams sit their best players and let unproven guys have playing time, Rubin was apparently strutting around like a rooster. He told the Sixers they were going to be great, that they were going to give the Celtics and the Knicks a run for their money in the East, and that all the great teams in the league were overrated. Nobody on the team could believe it. They all saw plain as day the Sixers weren't nearly as talented as those teams. Besides, these were exhibition games. Did Rubin know *anything* about pro basketball?

When the true season began and the losses started piling up, so did the mistakes from Rubin and Sixers GM Don DeJardin. Together, they rode a doomed carousel of misguided, impulsive roster alterations, trading players away on whims and bringing in over-burdened role guys in their place, advertising them as saviors of the ailing team. Their moves never made the team better, either. Rather, they just impeded consistency and cohesion.

As an in-game coach, Rubin was incoherent and almost clown-ish. He'd consider a pass "bad" if the player who received it didn't make the shot, and one time he pulled a muscle jumping off the bench to protest a call. His scouting, tactics, and leadership were almost profoundly poor, and so little did he inspire trust that his players actually met in secret after 35 games to stage a mutiny. In that meeting—you can imagine it taking place deep in the bowels of the Spectrum, the Philadelphia arena—the players decided to follow the lead of veteran guard Kevin Loughery instead, then they just went on that way, playing through the first 50 games of the year in rebellion against their bumbling bosses.

Despite the routine mismanagement and epic losing streaks, Rubin's guaranteed contract and tight relationship with DeJardin kept him on the Sixers until the All-Star Break, when Philly hit a record of 4-47. Only then did the team's owner, Irv Kosloff, give Rubin the axe.

Perhaps as an apology to the players, Kosloff instilled Kevin Loughery as interim player-coach after Rubin's dismissal. It was a good choice. Loughery was secretary of the NBA Players' Association and one of the most popular guys in the league. Even if he couldn't right the ship, he could at least maintain an atmosphere of respect, competitiveness, and dignity.

***

Showing up to Philly amid all that context felt a little like being dropped off at the Titanic after it had hit the iceberg. The trauma was over. The ship had sunk. I just dropped into the water and drifted about with the other survivors. Boy, was that water cold.

Yet I was surprised to find that instead of a bunch of shivering, discontent, spiteful men, the 76ers made up one of the most unified, spirited locker rooms I experienced in the pros. It seemed that even after all that had happened, most of the guys were gelling just fine! I went around the locker room and shook hand after hand and said hello to smiling face after smiling face. *What was going on here?* Kevin Loughery himself took me aside after the introductions.

"Good to have you, Tom." Loughery had a real thick New York accent, but he proved averse to hard discipline, and he didn't take himself too seriously as the coach. His handshake was enthusiastic and genial.

"Thanks, Coach. It's good to be here." I found myself smiling. I liked this guy.

Loughery waved me off. "You don't have to say that. It's been a tough year. But we know you have a good attitude, and that's what we want to maintain."

"I can do that."

"I know you can. You're an Indiana guy. What's the phrase? 'We got a lot of horseshit around here, so we might as well make some fertilizer?'"

I laughed. *Hey, that wasn't too far off from my mom's clover in the cow pasture!*

Loughery smiled. "Look, at the end of the day, just do your best, and every time you touch the ball, take the shot. We just want you to shoot, shoot, shoot."

I actually laughed again. "Really?"

"I'm not kidding." Loughery shrugged. "Shoot as much as you want. We need your scoring."

I grinned. "Whatever you say, Coach." *Hey, this might not be so bad!*

I took the floor that night in my Sixers debut, and I scored 24 points on 11 of 12 shooting. We lost. Then we lost nine more games in a row to fall to 4-59 and cement a 21-game losing streak. It was more than two weeks before I saw a win in a Sixers uniform.

***

In professional sports, bad teams come with complex diagnoses. Oftentimes, there are a number of root causes that contribute to poor performance. At a basic level, bad teams usually have a talent deficit compared with other teams in the league. The 1972-73 Sixers were a revolving door of cast-offs and role players, installed by a management group that had about the same knack for organizational construction as a kid running a lemonade stand. Interior size and physicality were paramount to a successful basketball team back then, but our centers—LeRoy Ellis and Manny Leeks—didn't have the stature you'd hope for, or the technical skills and bulldozer attitudes to compensate. They were great guys, but they were almost too nice to play in the NBA. Same went for our young players. Freddie Boyd, the team's first-round pick that year from Oregon, had a lot of talent, but was a little too timid against the physicality of the veterans, and meanwhile Dale Schleuter, our 6'10" center out of Colorado State, was more interested in being a goofball than cleaning the glass (though he was easily the funniest man on the team). The truth is, our Sixers just didn't have the overall talent to compete with most other teams, and the guys on the team who had talent at one point had lost it long before 1972.

The most famous player on the Sixers was Hal Greer, the 14-year pro, 1966 NBA champion, and future Hall-of-Fame point guard. It was Greer's final season. He played just 38 games. That was a little sad for me personally, because Greer was integral to a formative moment of my rookie season.

Back when I was on the Pistons, the 76ers were perennial championship contenders, one of those teams that put stars in my eyes as a young pro. Greer was the Sixers' starting point guard, surrounded by living legends like Billy Cunningham, Wilt Chamberlain, and coach Jack Ramsey. I was anxious to play in front of those guys, but not daunted. I matched up against Greer in my first game ever against Philadelphia. He was feisty, but I wasn't about to roll over.

I had some early opportunities with the ball, and as the game began, I actually attacked Greer on a couple drives. He was smaller than me, so I could finish through his defense if I had a strong first step. He didn't take much to contact. After I made a couple contested layups, he started glancing at the referees, as if to ask: *Are you seeing this nonsense?* I ignored the implication. That was the best way I knew how to succeed.

My next turn with the ball, I drove again at Greer, but he anticipated my drive and stayed in front of me. No problem. I crossed over and elevated for a jump shot, and Greer contested with his right hand, going for the block. Too late. I had him on my release, but as I let the ball fly, I felt something smack the top of my sneaker. *Woah!* It surprised me. I didn't finish my shot well and it clanked off the rim. *What was that?*

A few possessions later, I tried another shot on Greer. I thought I had him, but again, when I released, there was a *smack* on top of my sneaker. Miss. What was going on?

As we hustled back up the court together, I saw Greer smiling. He winked at me. "You lose your touch, rook?"

I realized what he was doing. As I was jumping up for my shot, he'd try the block with his right hand, *but swing down with his left hand and slap the top of my shoe.* It was a wily move. The referee would never catch it because they'd be watching Greer's other hand for a foul on my shooting arm. I was a little heated. It felt like a dirty move.

I didn't quit, though. The next time I went up for a shot, Greer smacked my shoe again (and I missed again—c'mon, Tom), so I came down and gave him a piece of my mind:

"Hal, if you do that again, I swear I'm going to kick the shit out of you."

Greer just laughed. "Listen, rookie," he said. "This isn't like high school or college. No one's going to protect you because you're Mr. Basketball this or All-American that. Here, you have to look out for yourself." As we reached the other end of the court, he gave me a nudge with his elbow. "I like your attitude, though. It'll take you a long way in this league."

In the pros, you see lots of questionable behavior with guys pushing boundaries and testing what they can hide from the officials, but it's really just a symptom of competition and survivalism. Everyone is so good in the NBA; you have to do everything you can to find an edge. With this in mind, I like to think in hindsight that in a sense, Hal Greer was complimenting my game by giving me the shoe-slap. He needed to dig into his bag of tricks to stop my scoring!

(And I will say, after I barked at him, he didn't smack my feet again.)

Imagine that player—a legendary, hard-working, savvy pro—riding the pine for one of the worst teams in history. I don't blame Greer if he ever felt spurned and unappreciated in 1972. He had given a title and most of his career to Philadelphia, and that was a difficult goodbye for him. Professional athletes want to go out on their terms, anyway—think of all the modern guys who have "retirement tours"—no one wants their final NBA season to be a lowlight. Greer's last season was literally the worst of his career. That's tragic. But he stuck around, mentored us, doled out wisdom, and when he saw the court, he worked his tail off. I admire that. Greer's attitude turned out to be indicative of the entire 76ers team that year—weary, but proud.

That probably surprises people who only see those Sixers for our record, but I understand that. Bad teams often harbor toxicity. The players and other personnel, in the face of adversity, sometimes abandon their collective mission in favor of mistrust, resentment, and selfishness. That's part of surviving in the NBA—when things become tough, you have to look out for Number One. But our team wasn't like that at all. From loss number one to loss number 73, we encouraged one another. It's hard to explain how.

***

One tangible source of morale on the Sixers, I can say, was our trainer, Al Domenico. Al was a longtime Philadelphia guy and a classical Italian. He was always slapping backs and shaking hands and flashing his carefree, boyish smile. He could've been 35, or 1,035. He was timeless, energetic, and irrepressibly enthusiastic. Everyone loved him.

I know the losing season was hard for Al because of his local fame. He had to field questions about the team everywhere he went. I have to think that fatigued him somewhat, but I can only guess, because inside the organization, he was always eager to give encouragement, lighten the mood, and make guys feel better. He sure made me feel great. He kept saying I was the easiest guy he ever trained, because I was one of the few guys on the team who didn't have his ankles taped. We'd laugh about that. But regardless of our demands on his time, Al always went the extra mile. Amid a season when most efforts seem futile, that was something.

I realized how far Al sometimes went to help the team one night late in the 1972 season. We were at home, and after I arrived at the arena for the game, I headed toward the locker room to prepare for warmups. I passed Al's training office and gave him a wave, but he held up his hand to stop me. "Tommy! How you are doing?"

Al was the only guy who could call me Tommy. "Just fine, Al." I stepped into his office and shook his hand. "I'm feeling good."

Al put his hands on his hips and nodded up at me, eyes wide with excitement. "Oh, terrific. Great to hear. We really need you out there tonight, Tommy. You know," he grabbed my arm and leaned in. I bent down. Al's voice lowered to a hush. "I always tell people who ask me, they say, 'Al, who's the best player on the Sixers?' and I say, 'No question, it's Van Arsdale.'" He beamed at me. "So, if you're good to go tonight, Tommy, we're good to go tonight."

I almost blushed. "Aw, well thanks, Al. We're gonna do the best we can. Let's get after it and get the win."

"You got it, Tommy."

I left the office with my chest out and my chin up, feeling like an MVP.

A few minutes later, I was changing in the locker room when Freddie Carter showed up. He was the team's leading scorer (I was second, but who's counting?), and he was usually pretty positive. His outlook that afternoon, however, seemed sunnier than usual. Freddie swaggered into the locker room. He waved at me. "Tom! It's going to be a good one tonight, I'll tell ya."

I raised my eyebrows. "Hey, Freddie. You seem well today"

"I sure am," Freddie chuckled and busied himself with his bag. "You know, we got ourselves a great trainer."

"Funny you should mention it, Al just gave me the nicest pep talk on my way in."

Freddie looked up. "No kidding? He was just hyping me up, too."

That was a little funny. "Oh, yeah?" I asked. "What's he think about the team?"

Freddie paused. "Well, he says we have some nice talent."

"Oh yeah?"

"Mhmm." Freddie seemed to think that folding his shirt was now the most engrossing thing in the room. "He, uh, loves the scoring ability of the starters."

I hid my smile. "Really? Any starters in particular?"

"Uh…no, not really." Freddie was blushing bad. And I knew what Al had told him.

"Well, you know Freddie, I think Al's dead on the money."

"You do?"

"Sure. Every other roster in the league only has one Best Player on the Team. It sounds like Al thinks we have two!"

We laughed a lot about that, but we decided we'd never confront Al about his little repetitious pep talks. That was his way of keeping us motivated and proud during a season when we didn't have much practical reason to compete. For the

160

remainder of the season, he kept puffing both of us up—*Freddie, you're the best player on the team; Tom, if we lost you, we'd be done for*—and we let him. Al needed a way to contribute, too, and let's be honest, it felt pretty good hearing before each game.

***

On the other hand, if there was one exception to the Good Ol' Boys on the Sixers that year, it was John Quincy Trapp. He was about as grouchy as his name suggested (though his name also suggests he was a crooked police captain or a Civil War general, but that's neither here nor there), and nobody liked him. Trapp was a chief complainer, and almost artful user of curse words. If the 76ers had a swear jar, he would've pitched in enough for us to buy the team off of Kosloff. Heck, he taught *me* some new words.

Trapp always had something to criticize, and a counterproductive know-it-all is one of the worst people you can have on a bad team. It's not leadership; it's just negative. There's that old business adage that says, "don't point out a problem without offering a solution." Well, Trapp not only could've used that one, he could've used the business adage that says, "don't drink bourbon out of a paper cup when you're sitting on the bench," too, but I guess he missed that one (seriously!). When you're losing as much as we were, you don't need anyone in your foxhole reminding you how bad things are. We know. We're right there with you.

I have one nice story related to John Quincy Trapp. It was late in the season, and we were on a road trip, boarding the team bus to head to the arena. I arrived early with Freddie Carter, and we were sitting in the back, chatting, as the rest of the team trickled onboard. After a while, we noticed two people missing—Coach Loughery, and John Trapp. Some of the guys started whispering. Freddie nudged me. "You think everything's okay?"

"I don't know," I said. "You think Trapp is giving Loughery a hard time about something?"

Freddie shrugged. "I don't know. Trapp hasn't seen much PT lately. Maybe that's it."

We waited a few minutes more. Before too long, Loughery appeared, alone. He jogged to the bus and climbed on and stood at the front and raised his hand for quiet. He looked flushed. Everyone piped down.

Loughery raised his eyebrows and let out a long breath. "Guys, I have an announcement to make." He paused and glanced out the bus window. Everyone waited. Then, Loughery cracked a grin. "I just told John Trapp he was cut. He's not on the team anymore."

There was a beat as the news sank in, and then the whole bus—every single one of us—burst into applause. Guys hooted and pumped their firsts, and after a few seconds, Freddie stood up, directing his claps at Loughery and whistling like he was at a Broadway play. Hal Greer followed Freddie's lead and stood up, too. Soon, we were all giving Loughery a standing ovation. In my opinion, it was his finest moment as our player-coach, maybe even the highlight of our season. I still admire that decision. Trapp had been such a negative influence, and Loughery wouldn't let him spoil the barrel, so to speak, 70-plus losses or not.

When Freddie and I sat back down, Freddie leaned over to me: "I'll follow our coach anywhere."

I had to agree.

***

Freddie Carter was my closest friend in Philadelphia. We had similar spirits to our game. He was the kind of guy who'd take it right at you in a practice scrimmage, knock you clean over, and after finishing the play, turn around and help you right up: *Hey, sorry Tom! I got you on that one, but if I gotta do it again, I will.* Freddie loved to score and loved to hustle. That made you want to cheer for him. No one had a problem with him leading the team in scoring, because Freddie himself had no ego. His success was our success. He just worked his tail off.

I look back on Freddie's time with the Sixers as a bit of a cursed existence—how did someone as competitive as him maintain the energy to lead us when we fell short so often? It's hard to make sense of, but it's inspiring, too. Freddie loved basketball, enough to where it was worth it to give his best every game no matter what. I felt that way, too.

It feels important to underscore here, finally, that the 1972 season was not sunshine and rainbows, no matter how many Al Domenicos and Kevin Lougherys we had in the organization. In a basketball sense, it's a difficult season to reflect on, and that's unfortunate because that's the primary way people want me to reflect about it. I still receive calls from the media about this team, and it's the same question over and over: *What was it like to have the worst record in the history of the NBA?* I don't take questions like that anymore. I have pride in my career. What do those reporters expect me to say, anyway? Losing isn't fun. There's no profound revelation here.

I must admit, though, as someone who's weathered their share of losses, 1972 felt a little different than other losing seasons. At every stop of my NBA career, I can compartmentalize the fun and the high jinks from the basketball disappointments, but it's hard to do that with my time in Philadelphia. Losing permeated our experience so much it bled into almost everything else in our lives. You couldn't close it off because to everyone who wasn't in the locker room, it was the entire story of the team. The losing defined us to the outside world, and in those circumstances, the definition began to subsume our personal identities.

I remember taking the floor before each game to warm up, just feeling downright embarrassed. I couldn't help it. I knew our record. I knew the other team knew our record. I knew the fans knew our record. It felt like I had regressed into the mentality of my Pistons years, when I had to prove I belonged in the NBA. The difference was, I had to prove it to everybody else instead of myself. That felt humiliating. I was in my prime. I was an All Star. My status should be more secure than that.

That insecurity didn't stay in the arena, either. Philadelphia has a proud sports tradition, with passionate, demanding fans. I'd leave the arena and on my way home, people would recognize me—a curse of being 6'5"—but instead of the good-games and back-pats I'd receive in Indiana, Detroit, or Cincinnati, people would hardly know what to say. What *could* they say? A few people offered encouragement: *Keep after it, Van.*

Next time, Van. I'd nod and say thank you and feel uncomfortable.

Practicing after a loss felt futile. *Here we go again. Why are we even here?* It felt like showing up to a corporate job knowing the business was losing money; it was hard to feel the passion for the work, the fire.

Those feelings fade for the most part—maybe some of the broader frustrations with losing remain—but in hindsight, I still feel terrible about my home life during this period. Kathy and I were together, and it was wonderful to be with her instead of going it alone in Philly, but this season was a huge challenge for our relationship. The losing streaks aside, game days were lost time for me regardless. My focus was always on staying rested and ready to play, and that meant the impetus was on Kathy to take care of the house, me, and eventually our children while I kept off my feet. I'd rest, nap, *maybe* go out to run an errand or two, but by and large, I'd be a slug until about 3:00 in the afternoon, when I'd move to our dining room table to eat the early dinner Kathy would cook and serve for me. Then I'd leave for the arena. That was it.

Kathy would be the first to tell you she was miserable. To be the wife of a basketball player before the days of huge contracts, private chefs, and full-time nannies took grit and loyalty, and I'm amazed how Kathy sacrificed for me. She changed her whole lifestyle. Looking back, I'm humbled how she worked to serve our family while I chased my NBA dream. She's special for that. I don't tell her often enough how much I appreciate it.

***

165

People expect every story about the 1972 76ers to be like that. The hangdog tales are still the ones that seem to stick in the record books, and that's an unfortunate symptom of sports media. A team that finishes 9-73 is a plain old losing team, and that's the end of it.

But in my memory, that Philly team isn't a bunch of losers. Not even close. I actually become defensive if you press me on this: Anyone on that Philly team will tell you that no matter how bad it became, no matter how many games we lost, we always thought we had a chance to win the next one. We were a positive, unified, hopeful group. It's a private legacy, but it means a lot to me. It represents how much I changed over the course of my career.

I used to question my place in the league. I used to wonder if I was good enough to play alongside my heroes. I used to give 110 percent just to prove to myself that chasing a pro basketball career was worth the effort. In Cincinnati, I finally received the affirmation and esteem I needed to feel secure with myself, and in Philly, that esteem saved me. Amid the misery of an all-time losing season, I held fast to the knowledge there were peers and coaches who respected me and admired me as a person and player, who recognized my effort and thought I was important. It's one of the most valuable changes in my life. It empowered me to turn my focus outward and pay more attention to the people I could influence in turn. I could give another pro the sense of belonging I felt, encourage someone who wanted to be where I was in my career, and be an example for them. That kind of empowerment only comes from difficulty. It comes from people carrying you through the difficulty. A pastor once told me you can't change without love. I think that might be true.

In the NBA, the pros who change teams a lot are called journeymen. Sometimes, you hear "journeyman" in a derogatory sense, but I've come to admire these players. They're resilient. They're tough. They don't take the gift of pro basketball for granted. I find a lot of kinship with that attitude. Winning makes life easy, because when things are going well, you're not likely to change anything and interrupt the patterns that gave you success. Change, self-imposed or otherwise, is what complicates your life. Journeymen have the most difficult careers in pro sports. They're the people without permanent homes, the people who play through injuries because their next contract isn't guaranteed, the people who extend their careers on things like hustle, sportsmanship, mentorship, and chemistry. Journeymen are dependable and rock-solid, but they can't depend on much themselves. They don't have the luxury of choices. Having choices, as a pro, is a privilege.

I didn't choose to be traded to the 1972 Philadelphia 76ers. No one on the team, certainly, chose to lose 73 games. But we never tanked or gave up or phoned in a performance. We won just nine games, but hell, we earned those nine games. That's life. There's still pride in the earning. Our tendency as people, when something bad happens to us, is to lower our heads and put ourselves down, but no one on our team did that in 1972. We had to learn to put our shoulders back and put our heads up and keep walking. And we did.

***

Thinking about this season reminds me of my granddaughter, Minna. She's 3 years old. Minna has Rett syndrome, a malformation of the X chromosome that leads to severe physical, mental, and developmental impairments. Only 1 in 10,000 little girls have it.

Minna won't grow up like other kids. She's a little behind on walking, and things like talking and even breathing might be more difficult for her than for other children. But Minna keeps going. She crawls around on her knees. She socializes. She enjoys being around people even if she can't talk with them yet. She likes to sit with you and look at you, and one of my favorite things to do is hold her and look her in the eyes and have a little staring contest. I always wonder what she's thinking about. She has the most beautiful smile.

Sometimes you're not treated fairly. Sometimes life hands you things you would never choose. But you find good in those things anyway. I'm 77. How many people—how many pro athletes—can say they were traded to a 4-47 team and come out the other side with stories like I have? The blessings in your life never look like what you expect. I'm happy. I wouldn't trade my blessings for anybody's.

Chapter Ten

A lot of books and movies say that when you hear about a death in your family, time stops. You lose track of where you are or what you're doing, maybe you drop something and it smashes on the ground in slow motion, you somehow lose your hearing. I didn't experience any of that on December 22, 1973, when I found out my dad died. Telling the story makes me feel almost self-conscious. I feel the loss more now than I did then.

I was with the 76ers in Portland to play the Trailblazers. It was the afternoon before the game, and Freddie Carter and I were resting in our hotel room when I got a message that said I had a call waiting in the lobby. I went down to take it.

After the operator connected me, I heard my mom's voice: "Tom?"

"Hi, Mom." I smiled. "How you doing?"

Mom kept her voice very calm. "Tom, it's about your dad."

My smile disappeared. "Okay."

"Your dad died today, Tom."

I heard the words as if someone had said them on the evening news. It seemed matter-of-fact, almost emotionless. "Okay," I said again. "Should I come home, do you think?"

"Tonight?"

"Yeah."

"You're supposed to play, aren't you?"

169

"Yeah."

"Your dad wouldn't want you to miss a minute, you know."

"Yeah, I know." My smile almost returned. "He'd hate if I took the night off."

My mom's voice lightened. "He would."

"Well I think I might stay and play the game, Mom."

"I think that's what your dad would want."

"And I'll come home after?"

"Sure. Come home after."

"Okay."

"Okay, Tom."

There was a pause. It felt like a fast conversation. Should this have taken longer?

"Mom?"

"Yes, Tom?"

"Are you okay?"

My mom thought for a second. "Oh, I'll be alright. Are you okay?"

I thought for a second. "Yeah, I'll be alright, too."

"I love you, Tom."

"I love you, too, Mom. Bye now."

"Have a good game."

And that was it. Dick says Mom called him right after.

I've looked up my statistics from the game against Portland that night. I scored 19 points, and I didn't shoot any better or worse than I normally do. On paper, it's a completely unremarkable game in my career, but that makes sense to me, because really, I was unaffected by the news from my Mom. I wasn't sad, I wasn't broken up, I wasn't even a little extra motivated to do well. There was no "let's win this one for Dad" (we lost to the Blazers by 5, for the record) or "Dad was watching over me, willing the ball into the basket." I just showed up and did my job and went home.

I loved my dad, but it was a different kind of love than one you have with a dad who's your best friend, or a dad who's always there when you need him. Late in my dad's life, he became very unwell. He was in and out of mental institutions in Indiana throughout my college and NBA years, receiving treatment for depression and alcoholism. And it wasn't treatment like people receive today. There was no Prozac or anything like that, no caregivers or counselors. No, they gave my dad rounds of shock treatment—electroshock therapy, two or three rounds at a time—before sending him home. The memories of visiting him in the institution are embedded in my mind. It looked like something out of *One Flew Over the Cuckoo's Nest*, or *Silence of the Lambs*. They had to buzz me into his ward, a long hall of rooms behind a locked gate. His room was like a cage, with bars on the window in the door. The isolation weighed on him, and what I remember most was how he just couldn't smile. He was proud of Dick and me for playing basketball in the NBA, but he couldn't bring himself to express any of that happiness. I felt awful for him.

Between treatments, Dad would just be lethargic in the house and drink a lot, and he was always sad. His decline was enormously difficult for Mom. Her attitude was as resilient as ever, but Dad was a burden on her when he was home. She had to spend most of her time taking care of him, and that put a lot of constraints around her life. She couldn't go watch Indiana basketball games or go to her bridge club. She couldn't do a lot of things she wanted to do. I don't blame Dad for that—he was suffering tremendously—but when he died, I know my mom felt free. She went back to Bloomington to watch the Hoosiers, and back to her bridge club, and she began filling her life up again. She was able to enjoy herself in a way she hadn't in years. When she started living on her own again, Dick and I made it a habit to call her every Monday night. She never missed a week, as if she was waiting by the phone.

My personal memory of Dad is colored in shades of gray. His open criticism against Dick and me always went hand in hand with his love for us. He walked home after our poor middle-school performance because he thought we weren't fulfilling our potential. He fell apart after our state championship loss because he was devastated for us. He bemoaned our decision to go to Indiana because he didn't want us to miss out on the NCAA tournament. He never let us forget a loss because he wanted so badly for us to succeed. Maybe he was putting too many expectations on us, or maybe he was living vicariously through us. Regardless, I know he cared for us very much.

During my own low periods, I sometimes wondered how much my Dad's pessimistic and self-critical attitude trickled down to me. When I wouldn't leave the bus at Manual, when I quit the Pistons' training camp, or when I took myself out of certain games because I thought I didn't belong—*was that my Dad's voice speaking to me?* When you internalize your failures—

when you go from "I made a mistake" to "I *am* a mistake"—that's shame talking, and when shame controls what you do and don't do, that's depression. Goodness knows I've experienced that kind of failure, and I've come to understand that my dad experienced that, too. It gives me a lot of empathy for him.

That's why I say I've actually grown a lot closer to my dad since his death. I understand how badly he was suffering now. His high expectations for Dick and me were really expectations he placed upon himself. He didn't have much of an identity outside of our achievements, and he couldn't escape that burden. Dad worked so hard. He was loyal to my mom, committed to us, always honest, and dedicated in a way that wasn't obvious at the time, but is clear as day now. I love him. I wish I could thank him.

I still hold one favorite image of my brother and me with Dad. In our early years of playing basketball, we'd come home from practice to find Mom cooking in the kitchen while Dad graded papers in his office. Dick and I were supposed to start our homework before we ate dinner with the family, but sometimes we'd head into Dad's office instead, and he'd ask us to help him grade papers. What a neat thing for a father and his twin sons to do! *Gosh, Dad wants our help with his job?* We couldn't believe it!

Dad would divide his papers into three stacks (now, I realize he was just trying to finish faster so he could listen to basketball on the radio, but I'll give him a pass for that), one for each of us, and Dick and I would take ours and start grading. The whole time, we'd be asking questions: *What's this kid like, Dad? And is this one smart? This one here didn't do well—is he a goof-off?*

And Dad would always tell us the truth! *Oh, she's very smart—respectful, too. But that other kid's lazy—if he studied, he'd do better. And yes, Stanley Meisterman is a goof-off, and if you met his parents you'd understand why!* My dad was a great teacher. When I go back to Indiana to this day, I meet people who recognize me and say, before anything about basketball, "Your dad was the toughest teacher I ever had, but you know, he was also the best." It's amazing. Whenever it happens, I think of those times we spent in his office, and I see why they all feel that way. Dad really knew each of his students. Behind the scenes, he gave a lot of himself. Behind the scenes, he was really going through some turmoil, too.

***

I admire and appreciate athletes who speak up about mental health challenges, because it's not an easy topic to breach in sports. A lot of modern male athletes are still stuck in traditional presentations of machismo and toughness, but on the other hand, more guys are sharing their struggles than ever before. I remember being depressed in the NBA and trying to hide it from my teammates. I was afraid sharing that part of myself would affect how they'd see me, especially considering I built my game on toughness and tenacity. Would they think I was weak? Soft? Would coaches take away my playing time or starting position if they knew I was depressed? Those were legitimate concerns for me.

Professional athletes face unique challenges when it comes to their mental health, often in a counterintuitive sense. A lot of people might think fame and visibility counters depression: *How can you be depressed when you have so many fans?* Well, that's the thing: Being put on a pedestal is exactly what makes being a pro athlete so hard on your self-image and outlook.

A pedestal is a lofty perch, but it's also narrow and unstable. You could fall at any moment. Some guys feel comfortable in the public eye, like Shaquille O'Neal or Charles Barkley, but I was always humbled by attention. I felt an enormous sense of pressure by being known. I felt like I had to be perfect all the time, and in the back of my mind I was constantly policing my own behavior. Would a waiter say something bad about me if he thought I didn't tip him enough? Would I lose my image if I flipped the bird to someone in traffic? Little social graces are inflated into sweeping indications of character when you're just a little bit famous.

And I never liked being revered. When people approach me and tell me what a great guy I am or say I was someone they admired when they (and I) were younger, it feels complicated. I sure appreciate it, but that adds to the pressure of having to live up to people's expectations. I find that's specific to professional athletes. Other professions can evoke performance anxiety or high-stakes competition, but only athletes have to display their success to the public, then concern themselves with maintaining it.

My personal depression was tied to that dynamic, because the person who had me the most on a pedestal, actually, was Dad. Each milestone of my career—the championship games, the barnstorming tours, the All-Star appearances—added new bricks atop the tower of his expectations, a higher platform from which I could tumble. Thank goodness I was surrounded by coaches and peers who assured me I was building a career to be proud of, and that I wasn't alone on the pedestal. What a relief. That's the irony of professional sports. Its camaraderie and fellowship make it the segment of popular culture most capable of talking about mental health, and yet, it still struggles to do so. Thank goodness that's beginning to change.

***

One of the most inspiring stories I ever witnessed in basketball was that of Maurice Stokes, whom I met during my time in Cincinnati. Stokes played for the Royals from 1955 to 1958, and wow, was he good. He was the NBA Rookie of the Year in 1955, an All-Star each season he was in the league, and a three-time All-NBA selection. His career was cut short, however, by a tragic incident in the last game of the 1957-58 season. Stokes was driving to the basket when he took some contact, fell, hit his head on the court, and blacked out. They had to revive him with smelling salts. A few days later, Stokes became violently ill, and within a week, he had a seizure that left him permanently paralyzed. He was diagnosed with post-traumatic encephalopathy, a brain injury that affects your motor-control center. He couldn't move his limbs, and he couldn't speak.

Jack Twyman was Stokes' teammate on the Royals, and after Stokes' injury, Twyman became Stokes' legal guardian at just 24 years old. At the time, it was an almost foolish act of generosity for Twyman—Stokes' medical bills were estimated to cost $100,000 per year, but Twyman only made $15,000 per year in the NBA. Somehow, that didn't deter him.

176

As Stokes began his recovery and rehabilitation, Twyman stuck by him. They developed a shorthand in which Stokes would blink his eyes at Twyman to communicate, and Twyman helped Stokes maintain his dignity and autonomy as they navigated the first year following the accident. It was an amazing partnership, but finances were still a problem. That's when a man named Milton Kutscher, a New York hotelier and basketball fanatic, offered his help.

Kutscher had a pitch for Twyman: a charity basketball game at his hotel in the Catskill Mountains to raise money for Stokes' treatment. Kutscher would provide the rooms and food if Twyman could recruit the talent. Twyman agreed, and the inaugural Maurice Stokes Memorial Basketball Game tipped off in 1959 featuring the likes of Bob Cousy, Wilt Chamberlain (who had actually been a bellhop at Kutscher's when he was young), Bill Russell, and John Havlicek. By the time I was on the Royals, participating in the game was a time-honored tradition for guys on the team, and I jumped at the chance to participate.

The weekend of the game, all the Royals who signed up to play met Stokes and Twyman at the airport. Stokes arrived on a gurney, and I and a couple other guys volunteered to wheel him up the jetway, right onto the plane. Stokes wasn't in good physical shape, obviously, but he was all there mentally. You could see he was right there with us, excited for the weekend away, and even more excited to watch basketball.

The Stokes game itself was nothing like a modern All-Star Game. We put on a show for the fans, sure, but we all took the competition seriously (especially Wilt, who seemed eager to be the hotel's hometown hero of sorts). The environment really encouraged us to give 100 percent. We played on an asphalt court flanked by wooden bleachers, under the lights and surrounded by rowdy New Yorkers. Kids ran all over the place. Parents oohed and ahhed. The younger adults...well, they loved being close to a bunch of famous athletes. It was the same idyllic atmosphere I had back in Greenwood, plus the rabid crowds I played for in high school and college. All us players really brought it. We went at each other and hustled and talked trash. We had a great time.

And I have to say this, too: These days a lot of charity functions pay stars to participate, but all of us played the Maurice Stokes game for free, and we were happy to do it. We had a blast supporting Stokes. I'll always remember him propped up courtside, grinning behind his glasses, watching the game.

Sports foster an environment of support unlike anything else in life. Your natural instinct as a teammate is to sacrifice for your peers, and your perspective is always oriented toward something greater than yourself: the team, the season, a championship. That breeds empathy. I don't know why more athletes don't speak up about mental health struggles because I don't know why an athlete's response would be anything except "I have your back." Sports is about picking each other up before it's about manning up. How did that become so twisted? How could I be scared to share my struggles in the NBA, the same place where we all came together for Maurice Stokes? I hope more pro athletes follow the footsteps of guys like Terry Bradshaw, Michael Phelps, Jerry West, Dak Prescott, and DeMar DeRozan, and keep talking about their mental health. Sports should be on the frontlines of that conversation. We could make an enormous difference.

***

In the timeline of my NBA story, we've reached 1974, when I was traded from the Philadelphia 76ers to the Atlanta Hawks. I was with Atlanta for two years, until 1976, but I don't have many basketball memories of the Hawks because, honestly, I felt more disassociated with Atlanta than anywhere else I played. There wasn't much local interest in basketball, and Kathy and I had a hard time finding community. I had a few friends on the Hawks, including my teammate Lou Hudson, one of the best guys I ever competed against in college or the pros, and Gene "Bumper" Tormohlen, our assistant coach and a fellow Indiana native, but there wasn't much to latch on to besides. I feel now like those years just sort of floated over my head.

The most important relationship I built in Atlanta was with our head coach, the future Hall of Famer Cotton Fitzsimmons. Cotton was like if you put a patterned jacket and wispy wig on a lean, wily jackrabbit. His smile never faded, his fire off the bench never cooled, and his aura never dimmed. He was such a strong, passionate presence, you almost had no choice but to like him. He'd just wear you down. There was a little history between us—he had coached Dick in Phoenix in the early part of the 1970s—and we took to one another fast. In Atlanta, he was just about the only thing keeping me tied to the ground.

On paper, my relationship with Cotton is tricky to describe, because we were much closer than the typical player and coach. Sometimes he was like a father to me. Other times, more like a brother. Obviously, that blurs some professional and personal lines, but nevertheless, Cotton and I talked about everything.

My move to Atlanta came at a significant time in my life. Kathy and I had only been married a few years, my father had just passed away, and my NBA career—my dream—was starting to close. My life was full of change, endings, and beginnings, and as it happened, so was Cotton's at the time. When I arrived in Atlanta, Cotton was going through a difficult divorce, and as our friendship grew, I became his confidant and support person. He didn't have much of a community in Atlanta, either, having been made coach only a few years earlier, so we connected. We talked about our previous marriages—I had been through a divorce before I met Kathy—and when he started seeing his second wife, JoAnn, I became close to them as a couple. It was valuable for both Cotton and me, I think to be able to compare those experiences.

Something I didn't understand about Cotton right away, however, was his Christian faith. He used to organize a prayer with a pastor before all of our games on the Hawks—the first pro coach I had who did that—and he was generally open about his values with the people he met. It wasn't aggressive or pushy, though. When Cotton combined his faith with his trademark energy, he carried an almost televangelist, holy roller vibe, and he'd sometimes bring his faith into our personal conversations about marriage and family life. Usually, his words about Jesus and the Holy Spirit and blessings would go right over my head, but something about them always appealed to me. I only understood what he meant after 1975, when my life changed forever on a beach at Coronado Island.

***

Growing up in Greenwood, Dick and I quit going to church as soon as Mom and Dad let us decide between going to service or basketball practice on Sundays. No brainer. Dad would be putting on his jacket and tie while we were putting on our sneakers. The best part was, in our parents' eyes, there wasn't really a wrong choice. They let us go without any comment or consequence or stipulation. It was our decision; they respected it.

That said, I was always a curious kid, interested in different worldviews and perspectives, so whenever I wasn't playing basketball, chances are I had my nose in a book. I read to learn things, so I usually picked something about history or philosophy instead of a novel. I loved it, and still do. Today, my personal library is one the proudest parts of my home (and it's not just basketball books—although, I have at least 200 of those, sorted by author and whether they're autographed).

I'm not sure what I wanted to learn as a kid, exactly, but when I tell this story, I find myself coming back to the phrase "looking for an answer." I was always looking for an answer, a better understanding of what life meant or what I was supposed to be doing. Playing basketball was fun and fulfilling, but…what was it all for? What was my purpose? I felt like so many things in my life were given to me by something bigger than the world, but what was that? Where did that feeling come from? I read and read and searched and searched, but nothing seemed to be able to explain all that.

181

I was still questioning my way through life when I entered the NBA. In Cincinnati, I met a trainer named Joe O'Keefe. Joe had a fascinating career trajectory. Before he became a trainer, he enrolled in seminary school down South to become a priest. He dropped out before finishing, but his Catholicism was still central to his life. He had a lot of knowledge of the Bible, invoked it often in his work, and prayed the rosary while we traveled on road trips (that was always a little goofy to me—saying the same prayer over and over—doesn't God hear it the first time?). But something must have drawn me to that posture, because when we had a day off on the road, Joe would find a local Catholic church to go pray, and sometimes I'd go along just to see what all the fuss was about. I wasn't Catholic nor Christian, but...I don't know, sometimes life just pulls you along like that.

I had an interest in faith, but in 1975, when Kathy and I were living in Atlanta and vacationing in Coronado during the offseason, nothing was real for me yet.

The particular day I'm remembering was a breezy, productively do-nothing vacation day. The sun shone on the beach in front of the Hotel Del Coronado, and you only heard the ruckus of the beachgoers if you paid attention. My chair was comfortable, an umbrella shaded my face, and Kathy was beside me. I had my nose in a book and not a care in the world.

The book was Hal Lindsey's *The Late Great Planet Earth*, which had sort of a moment in the 1970s. It was all about the future of the planet in connection to the prophecies found in the biblical Book of Revelation. It talked about climate change, conflict in the Middle East, and other things Lindsey argued could be signs of the apocalypse—*so you better figure out your life right now!* I know it sounds nuts 50 years later, but you have to remember, in the 1970s, it felt like the world was going to end any second. Vietnam was rife with war, the Soviet Union was stockpiling nuclear weapons, the President was paranoid, and the news was non-stop violence and protesting. *The Late Great Planet Earth* sold 15 million copies, and not just to Christians. People really thought the end of the world was coming!

But *the Late Great Planet Earth* also included an impassioned case for the reader to consider Christianity. This is the part I really remember. I can almost recall the exact words: "All you have to do to begin a relationship with Jesus is this: When you hear Him knock on the door, open it, and let him come into your life."

Huh. I thought. *It's that simple?* I was struck how there was no mention of earning enough karma or doing enough good deeds or saying enough prayers. *I just...open the door?* And as I thought about that—I swear this is true—I felt a heat wave begin flickering in my feet. The warmth spread, moving up my ankles, up my legs, into my chest. My fingers grew hot, and so did my arms. My throat felt like I had just had the world's most comforting cup of coffee. And the warmth wrapped itself around my head and seemed to just rise right out the top of me. It was...it was wonderful, really, but I was stunned. *What in the world just happened to me?* I couldn't explain it.

I turned to Kathy. "Hey, Kathy."

Kathy grunted. She was sunbathing.

"Kathy, you won't believe this."

My wife raised her sunglasses and looked at me. "What is it?"

"I just…this is going to sound funny." And I told her the whole story, from what it said in the book to what I was thinking to the electric hot feeling all through my body.

Kathy's a discerning, intelligent, grounded woman. She sat up. "Really?"

I nodded. I was becoming kind of excited. "Yes, really!"

And I don't know what it was in my face or my expression or just the trust Kathy and I had built up in one another, but she believed me, and I believed, too. I've been following Jesus ever since, and that faith has never gone away. When I think back on that feeling on the beach today, I truly believe it was the Holy Spirit changing my life.

***

Jesus could not have entered my life at a better time. Toward the end of your career as a basketball player, a strange insecurity sets in as you fight to maintain utility. Younger players come in with better legs and more energy and it's difficult to come to terms with your decline. When coaches notice you're losing a step and start changing how much you play, it feels disappointing because your past experience tells you that you have the ability to earn those minutes, just like you did when you were younger. It feels like your body's aging against your will, almost. It's not cooperating with the rest of you. In the wrong mindset, you can feel like you're letting yourself down.

But rather than wilt amid my so-called decline, my faith actually made me stronger. The Bible urges you to view things through an eternal lens, and that gives you a profound sense of peace with yourself. Your weakness is temporary, because God promises restoration. Your mistakes are forgiven, because God offers His grace. Your disappointments are fleeting, because God's working for your good in a way beyond your understanding. That, all together, is the peace of a relationship with Christ. No matter how bad I screw up or what kind of disappointments I face in life, I can rest in that peace knowing I am accepted, I am cared for, and I belong.

I've heard it said that when our circumstances don't match our expectations—heck, that's the story of my whole career in the NBA—we tend to turn inward and focus on ourselves. That tendency really troubled me before my relationship with Jesus, and that made it hard to see the bigger picture amid all the misfortune of my career. But faith introduced a stabilizing, peaceful presence in the middle of all that chaos. It was easier to have fun in basketball after I became a Christian, easier to focus on the things I loved about the NBA and the blessings the sport had brought to me. My faith reminds me, still, that no matter what happens around me, things will be alright. I hold on to that.

***

A misconception people have about Christianity is that after you confess your faith in Jesus, your journey stops. You accept your salvation, dust off your hands, and go on living however you want with Christ as your Get Out of Jail Free card. It doesn't work like that. The Bible describes a relationship with God as a living faith. It grows and matures and strengthens through life's trials. You grow in faith, God asks you to take a step with that faith, and when you do, God responds by moving in such a way that pushes you to keep growing.

It sounds simple, but I'll tell you, taking that step of faith is hard.

In the summer of 1976, Kathy and I were at home in Phoenix. I had just finished my second season with the Hawks, and Kathy and I had finished building our house on the side of Mummy Mountain. We were tangibly, memorably happy. I was preparing to go back to training camp in a few weeks.

But one night, someone with the Hawks gave me a call. It was another reprise of the matter-of-fact, life-altering sentence I had heard four times already: "Tom, we have traded you to the Buffalo Braves." There was nothing I could do. I thought, *You've got to be kidding me*, and the conversation was over before I could say much else. The team official hung up first.

After I hung up, Kathy must've seen the look on my face. "What was that, Tom?"

I shook my head. I always hated telling Kathy these things. It was such a disruption to her. How could she build a life when we were moving around so much? "Buffalo," I said. "I'm being traded to Buffalo."

"Oh no."

Kathy echoed exactly how I felt. I didn't want to play in Buffalo. No one wanted to play in Buffalo. It's like the Siberia of the United States. I looked out our front window at our mountainside view. *I wish I could make a different choice,* I thought.

But maybe I could.

Two days later, I received another call, this time from the Buffalo Braves. It was a trainer, I remember. Unbelievable. The first person to welcome me to my new team was a trainer. At least he was nice.

"Tom, we're so happy to have you up here in Buffalo," he said. "All we need is you to tell us which number you'd like on your uniform."

By then, I knew what I wanted. "You know what? Thanks, but no number."

The trainer actually blubbered. "W-w-w-what?"

"No number."

"You want the number zero?"

"No. No number at all. No jersey at all. Because I don't want to come to Buffalo. I'm going to retire instead. I'm ready to hang it up. No more uprooting my family. No more new cities. No more new jerseys or numbers or any of it. I'm done."

"What! Come on!"

But I had made up my mind. This was my next step. It was time to let go of basketball. I was at peace with my career. I was proud. I didn't need to go chasing any more playoff appearances or 40-point games or All-Star nominations. I was finished. I hung up with the trainer, and to this day I don't know what happened with the trade between the Braves and the Hawks. I assume it didn't go through, but regardless, I stumbled into the only way a player of my stature could stop a transaction in the NBA back then—just quit. I had followed the whims of other people my whole career. I was going out on my terms.

For the next few weeks, Kathy and I were as happy as we have ever been. We lived up in our beautiful new home, in that beautiful setting, talking about a life after the NBA. I was really looking forward to it. I could work with Dick after he retired, and we could go into business together and build ourselves a great life in Arizona. This would work out. This was going to be alright.

But then, another call.

Kathy and I were in bed (I was reading, of course) and the phone on my end table rang. I answered it, a little indignant someone was calling so late. "Hello?"

"Tom Van Arsdale. This is Jerry Colangelo."

I sat bolt upright. "Mr. Colangelo, absolutely. Hi. How are you?"

"I'm just fine. Listen, I have a question for you."

I glanced at Kathy. She was watching me. *It's Jerry Colangelo,* I mouthed. She jumped a little and leaned in toward the phone. "A question? Okay." I said.

"I hear you're set to retire, but if I could make a trade for your rights with the Hawks, would you be willing to take a pay cut to come play for me?"

My whole body felt supercharged. *Was this really happening?* I looked at Kathy, bewildered. She looked at me, bewildered. I nodded. She nodded. I mashed the phone back against my ear. "Jerry," I said. "How soon do you want me?"

He laughed. "That's what I like to hear. Welcome to the Phoenix Suns, Tom."

And just like that, impossibly, somehow, as if it had been the plan the whole time, I made it to my dream team. I was going to be teammates with my brother Dick. I was going to end my career in my favorite city, with my best friend, with my wife, happy. *Unbelievable.*

The best thing I ever did was retire early. My final year in Phoenix would be one of the happiest years of my life. I was home. I was where I belonged. After years and years of bouncing around the NBA, I landed. My feet finally touched the ground.

JOURNEY MAN

Chapter Eleven

The first time I smelled the orange blossoms, I knew I didn't want to leave Phoenix. The opportunity to see my brother Dick aside, Phoenix was always one of my favorite cities to visit on the road during a season. Something about the West has always had a sense of romance for me. I love the wide-open spaces (room to move freely is not always a given when you have pro-basketball height) and I love how the sun shines all year round. I love how the desert itself rises and falls and turns into mountains—I just had flat cornfields and maple trees in Indiana—and the desert's muted greens and blues and browns are just beautiful to me. The colors always struck me as humble until the sunset, when everything you can see is burned by oranges and purples and reds that don't seem possible in nature. This is an amazing place. From the moment I touched down here in Phoenix, I knew I didn't want to be anywhere else.

The greatest contrast between Arizona and the Midwest, however, proved to be the culture. Back east in the United States, there are established social hierarchies. The South has wealthy generational families with sprawling plantation homes, the East has industry titans, and the Midwest has its bluebloods, the institutions that present humbly but operate ruthlessly, like the Capone crime syndicate of Chicago. Most of America has an entrenched, permanent feeling history that's resistant to change, but the West doesn't answer to anything like that. It's been discovered and rediscovered for centuries now. People can come to places like Arizona and make themselves whomever they want, perceive the land any way they want. For me, someone whose life and career had always ebbed and flowed with forces greater than myself, it was liberating.

Most NBA superstars today gravitate toward major markets like New York, Boston, Los Angeles, and Miami, which creates a little bit of imbalance in the league in terms of where the good teams are and how they're built. But every now and then, a successful team appears in a smaller market like Memphis or Oklahoma City, and I find those teams typically have a special, organic collection of talent. Their chemistry is natural rather than synthesized in the front office. The Suns team I joined had this exact type of chemistry.

During the 1975-76 NBA season, the year before I joined the team, the Suns finished the regular season with a record of 42-40 and squeaked into the playoffs. However, thanks to the presence of that season's Rookie of the Year Alvan Adams and future Hall of Fame point guard Paul Westphal, the Suns went on an improbable playoff run all the way to the Finals. They upset the Seattle SuperSonics in the first round, who were coached by Bill Russell, and they shocked the top-seeded Golden State Warriors in the conference finals, a team led by Rick Barry. They faced the Boston Celtics in the Finals and took them to six games before losing the championship, but it was nonetheless a year of remarkable overachievement and exceeded expectations. The consensus was the next year—1976-77—the Suns would be legitimate title contenders.

All the hype was music to my ears. In fact, when Jerry Colangelo called me to ask me to join the team, he had said: "Tom, you're finally going to be on a winning team." I was thrilled.

The Suns had a talented roster during my year in Phoenix, but let's just say we weren't the flashiest group—more a bunch of goofballs and misfits than a professional basketball team.

The linchpin of our team, Alvan Adams, was a string bean 6'9" center who, though listed at 210 pounds, I ballpark south of 200. He was so thin I used to think one of the referees could knock him over, and he had floppy rock-band hair and enough sweat in him to make a racehorse wrinkle its nose. When I first saw Alvan I thought, *This guy's a first-round draft pick and Rookie of the Year? What is everyone talking about?*

Well, I found out quickly. Alvan was strong. He moved fast and decisively, like a jackrabbit, and he had a nonchalant disposition to his game that made him seem almost detached. He was never emotional on the floor. He didn't holler or yell when he wrestled a rebound from someone or drew contact going to the basket. He had one mode. He put his head down, competed, and scored like a machine.

There were more characters in the Suns' extended cast. Curtis Perry, our 6'7" starting power forward, was built like a bear, but he had the energy to match. Meanwhile, Keith Erickson was our resident old-timer, but he still had enough zip to try and compete with me for PT—we'd absolutely kick the shit out of one another in practice. Dale Schleuter, one of my old Philadelphia teammates, was our gangly, enthusiastic center, and he had arms like bucatini. Our coach, John MacLeod, hated Dale's arms. Whenever Dale would go up for a rebound in practice and clock somebody by accident, MacLeod would be on him: "Dammit, Dale. You're going to give somebody a concussion. This isn't a jazzercise class. Keep your arms to yourself."

Dale was a good, earnest guy. He'd just say: *Sorry, Coach. You got it.* And then he'd run down court with his arms pinned to his sides like a dinosaur.

Paul Westphal and Ronnie Lee were our starting and backup point guards, respectively, but they were exact opposites. Westphal was from California, beloved, with a scoring ability as natural as his tan and his sense of cool. He wasn't especially fast or athletic, but he made decisions on the court that helped the rest of us play a little better. He had the perfect charisma for a floor general.

Ronnie Lee, however, was a rookie. That's not bad in and of itself, but Ronnie was a rookie in how he talked and how he practiced and how he played. Being around him was like being around a kid on Christmas morning; he was always wound up. We veterans had a hard time keeping up with his unbridled go go go sometimes, and we'd wonder among ourselves how he stayed so wired. *What's that Ronnie Lee's secret?*

Early in the season, before practice one day, Alvan Adams and I were hanging out in the trainer's room. Alvan was having his ankles taped and I was kicking back, chatting with him, when Ronnie came bounding inside. "Alvan! Tom! Good to see you guys!"

We nodded at the rookie. "Hey, Ronnie."

"Man, it's going to be a heck of a time out there today, fellas." Ronnie chuckled and cocked his grin to one side of his mouth, like a scheming cartoon character. It almost seemed like it didn't matter to him if we answered him. He just needed to be doing something. "Man oh man," he said again. He hopped up onto a training table and stretched his long legs in front of him and leaned forward and grabbed his toes. He shook his knees out and scooted backward so he was sitting against the wall and he unshouldered a big gym bag he had hanging off his back.

Honestly, Ronnie was so twitchy and spazzy that Alvan and I couldn't take our eyes off him. Our conversation stopped and we watched the rookie go about his business. He didn't seem to notice us staring.

Ronnie unzipped his bag from end to end and opened it wide and began rummaging around. There were some jingles and clanks—what the heck? —and then he pulled out a bright red can of Coca-Cola. He grinned to himself and tapped the top and lifted the tab to pop it open. *Pst!*

Alvan glanced at me. I met his eye. He gave me the tiniest of head shakes. I couldn't believe it, either. Maybe we didn't know much about nutrition in the 1970s, but we knew Coca-Cola was just about the worst thing you could have before a practice.

We looked back at Ronnie just in time to see him tilt the can back and chug the Coke like it was a bottle of water and he had just run a marathon. After several long gulps and a very satisfied *ahhhhhh...* Ronnie crumpled the can and tossed it back in the bag. "Y'all have a good weekend?" he asked.

I saw Alvan consciously close his gaping mouth before he said: "Yeah...yeah, we did."

Ronnie grinned. "Cool. Just cool, man." And he picked up his bag once more and resumed rummaging. But this time, his hand emerged clutching a six-pack of powdered-sugar donuts.

Alvan was about ready to fall of the table.

Ronnie resumed his conversation. "I went to the movies this weekend. Y'all seen *Marathon Man?*" he asked.

I shook my head. Alvan was frozen. Ronnie took a big bite of donut. "Oh, *man.*" Ronnie's eyes went wide and he coughed a little and cloud of sugar burst from his mouth like smoke. "You guys gotta go. It's great." He took another huge bite and Donut #1 was gone. He reached for another. "Dustin Hoffman plays this guy Babe, and he's gotta stop these Nazis from stealing some diamonds…" Another powdery chomp. Ronnie's face looked like a felony in all 50 states. "…but the thing is Dustin Hoffman's brother…"

Alvan and I listened to Ronnie recount the entire plot of *Marathon Man,* uninterrupted, while he snarfed all six of those powdered donuts. When Ronnie was done with both his synopsis and his snack, he hopped off the table, arched his back until we heard a loud *pop!,* dusted off his hands (another puff of white), said "See you fellas out there!" and zipped right out. We were stunned.

Then we did see Ronnie out there, 10 minutes later, zooming all over the court on his sugar high like a Looney Toon. He never crashed, and he never stopped. That Coca-Cola and those six donuts were his pre-practice ritual, every single day.

***

It would've been a headache to manage such a roster of knuckleheads, but lucky for us, the Suns' biggest character of all was John MacLeod, our head coach. MacLeod had a humble basketball career. He grew up playing in Indiana and saw some time at tiny Bellarmine University in Kentucky, but he was too short—just 6 feet—to have pro potential. He went into coaching instead, and there, his instinct for working with athletes emerged.

MacLeod didn't motivate us so much with his talk (he'd often shout himself into a nonsensical tizzy at halftime, spinning comical word salads like, "Don't let 'em keep…fuckin'…holding ya!") as much as his example. He was an overachiever—a pro head coach after just six years of experience at the college ranks, and an NBA Finals berth at age 38—so he inspired us to overachieve as well. I hate to admit this, but when I joined the Suns in 1976-77, MacLeod was just six years older than me. I was 33.

But let's be clear, MacLeod was not our peer, nor was he our buddy. He could be a real hard-ass when he wanted, though a more generous way of saying it might be: John MacLeod was very precise. One of his more infamous rules was we all had to simply be on time for the bus. I know that doesn't seem unusual—pretty much every coach has a "be on time" rule—but in a league where players are often given a little bit of special treatment, MacLeod actually enforced what he decreed. On other teams, the bus could be set to leave at 6:00, but you could show up at 6:04 or 6:05 certain it would still be there, waiting for you.

Not with MacLeod. He didn't wait for anybody.

When John MacLeod said the bus was going to leave the hotel at 5:00, you better be on the bus with your butt touching the seat at 5:00 or you'd miss MacLeod hollering, "Let's go, bus driver!" before he shut the doors and left you behind. You had to be early to the John MacLeod bus. Everyone was clear on this, but sometimes, guys became a little lackadaisical.

We were in Detroit. It was 4:59, and everyone was on the bus except one person: Curtis Perry, our starting power forward. As I mentioned: Curtis wasn't the fastest-moving guy on the team.

We all had our eyes on our watches as the second hand inched to the top of the hour. Dick and I held our watches together. I looked from his watch face to my watch face to the door of the hotel and back again. Watch, watch, door. Watch, watch, door. Fifteen seconds left...now twelve seconds...10 seconds...

Curtis Perry appeared on the other side of the rotating glass doors. "There he is!" someone shouted, and we all rushed to that side of the bus. Was he going to make it?

John MacLeod glanced up and checked his own watch with a flourish. "He better hurry."

9...8...7...

Curtis pushed open the hotel door, seemingly oblivious to the time. He had his sunglasses on, his bag at his side, and one of the hotel towels draped over his shoulders. He started toward the bus, but then, a small little girl—probably just 7 or 8 years old—ran up to him from the other side of the driveway, pen and paper in hand. *Oh no!*

Curtis saw the girl and stopped. He glanced at the bus and he held up his hand to ask us to wait. The seconds were ticking. *6...5...4...*

We all looked at MacLeod. It was time. He stood up and peered past us to look at Curtis, who was now kneeling in front of the little girl, smiling and saying something that made her blush and swivel around like kids do when they feel shy.

MacLeod frowned. "Let's go, bus driver!"

And with a hiss and a squeal, the bus driver closed the doors and released the brake. Curtis' eyes grew wide and he jumped to his feet. "No no no no no!" He shoved the pen and paper back in the little girl's hands and sprinted toward us, but the bus was moving. Curtis smacked the side with his free hand. "Hey! I'm here! I'm here!" But the bus only sped up.

Inside, we were just egging on the driver. *Step on it, bus driver! Let's get the hell outta here! No time to waste, bus driver!* We picked up speed, faster than Curtis could run, and we outstripped him at the end of the driveway.

"Nooooooo!" Curtis yelled. "Come on!" And we left him there alone in the street, panting, throwing his hands into the air.

MacLeod turned around and looked back at us from his seat up front. By this point, we were all beside ourselves with laughter. MacLeod smiled. "Thanks for being on time, gentlemen."

Curtis ended up taking a cab. He had to pay out of pocket (we all hated when we had to do that), and when he arrived at the arena, he was still muttering and steaming about it. Ronnie Lee went over to him. "Hey, Curtis."

Curtis huffed. "What is it, Ronnie?"

Ronnie grinned. He held up a pen and paper. "Could I have your autograph? I heard you never say no to meeting a fan."

***

I think any team that overachieves like those Suns does so out of a special sort of chemistry. Each man played their role perfectly during the Finals run in 1975—Alvan the unassuming star, Westphal the score-happy guard, Curtis Perry the bruising rebounder, and my brother Dick the off-ball hustler and shot maker. In 1975-76, the Suns had seven players average double figures in scoring on a per-game basis, but just one person (Westphal) had over 20 per game. That's a fantastic sign of ego-free distribution, each guy knowing his role and wanting to do as much as he could to help the team win. There was no hero ball, no "getting mine," and no feeding one man to "keep him happy." These guys put the group above themselves.

Stepping into that chemistry as a newcomer can feel a little tenuous. You don't want to disrupt the dynamic that made the team successful. But I found I had a kinship with many of the guys in Phoenix. We had a good foundation already through my relationship with Dick—he'd take me out with the Suns whenever I was on the road in Phoenix—so I knew players like Westphal and Erickson and Ricky Sobers before I joined the team. And I had been living in Phoenix during the offseason for a few years, so I had made friends that way. Really, I had been a Sun in every way except the official way for some time.

But beyond that establishment, everyone on that team was a self-starter just like me. There were no egos to be found, no one who thought they had the right to command the locker room and control how the rest of us played. Everybody just worked hard, paid attention to MacLeod, and hustled. The best evidence of our like-mindedness in 1976-77: We were third in the league in defensive rating. With our roster, you know that came out of discipline and consistency.

The easiest way to measure success is wins, but that's where our team faltered. After the magic of 1975, the Suns were expected to take a leap forward from their 42-40 record, but it seemed whatever genie, wizard, or witch had cast a spell over the team had called it quits. Instead, it felt like a cursed season. Alvan came down with a freaky case of strep throat and was only full-strength for about 40 games. He lost 20 pounds from his illness, and he didn't have much weight to lose in the first place. He was so weak, MacLeod wouldn't start him.

Curtis Perry, another starter, only logged 44 games in 1976 due to injury, and our other starting forward, Garfield Heard could only muster 46 games himself. Those two, along with Alvan, made up our entire starting frontline—the 3, 4, and 5 today—and they were gone not long after training camp. It was hard for the rest of us to make up for their absence.

This meant I had to play a lot more during my final season than expected—almost 20 minutes per game—but the injuries also felt like one last cheap shot from the fates about never playing for a winning team. The Suns finished 34-48 in 1976, well outside the playoffs. My peculiar legacy of scoring more points and playing more games than anyone who never made a postseason was secure.

I used to say missing the playoffs was the biggest regret of my career. But that implies I had full control over the matter. I didn't. It's not a regret I live with, just a disappointment.

***

Sometimes when I indulge in my lack of team accomplishments in the NBA, I think of a friend named Connie Hawkins. We were teammates for a short time in Atlanta, but he also spent time on the Suns, so I used to see him in Phoenix during and after our basketball careers. The Hawk became a legend well before we met, however—he's one of the most infamous players in NBA history.

Connie Hawkins emerged as a basketball superstar on the streets of New York City. He was a dominant presence on the famous Rucker Park court in Harlem, where other greats like Tiny Archibald, Julius Erving, and Earl Monroe also gained prominence as amateurs. Connie was a basketball trailblazer. He had a sensational, swooping, above-the-rim style of play—it was rare, then, to see an aerial specialist among basketball's typical ground-and-pounders—and many will tell you his athleticism equaled Erving, Chamberlain, or even Jordan. But the tragedy of the Hawk is that he missed most of his prime.

In 1961, Connie enrolled at the University of Iowa to play basketball. At the time, freshmen weren't allowed to play for collegiate varsity teams, so the Hawk sat out a year, waiting his turn. But during that season, college basketball became embroiled in an ugly point-shaving scandal, in which gamblers were paying players to affect the outcome of games.

Investigators connected The Hawk to one of the fixers, but Connie fervently denied the allegations—he wasn't even eligible to play! Nonetheless, the University of Iowa expelled Connie, the rest of the NCAA barred him from any other scholarships, and NBA commissioner James Walter Kennedy barred the Hawk from the pros as well. It was a basketball death penalty.

Forced to the outskirts of the sport, Connie settled for a year in the American Basketball League (he won MVP), then two years with the Harlem Globetrotters, then two years in the ABA (In 1968, Connie won the ABA's MVP and playoffs MVP awards, leading the Pittsburgh Pipers to a championship). Connie was so much better than everybody in those leagues, it was almost an insult to himself and his peers not to have him in the NBA. He was born to be an all-time great.

In 1969, new evidence in the point-shaving case against Connie confirmed he had no part in the scandal, and the NBA finally dropped their ban, paid him a cash settlement, and let him into the league. The Suns picked him right up. Connie was 27, at the end of his prime, and all but devastated by the emotional trauma of his career thus far. Still, he had accomplished his dream—he was in the NBA.

When the record books closed, the great Connie Hawkins had just seven NBA seasons to show for himself. He had a strong career—he was a top-10 scorer and first-team All-NBA in 1969-70—but it was inevitably dogged by what-ifs.

Connie had, without question, the worst luck of any player to ever aspire to the pros. Some say he was the greatest basketball player who ever lived. But we'll never know. He didn't have the same opportunities as everyone else.

Given all that he had been through, Connie had an uncommon ease about him in person. I have trouble explaining it to this day. For someone so afflicted, he always seemed so at peace. He was famous and in demand, but he had a knack for blending in, letting life play out, and making you feel comfortable just sitting back and watching it go right along with him. Connie's demeanor reminds me of the regality seen in legends like Bill Russell and Kareem Abdul-Jabbar. He was elegant, observant, thoughtful, and measured. I loved being around him.

I never heard Connie talk about what happened to him before the NBA, and that's always struck me. He had every reason in the world to be bitter, resentful, pissed off, and spiteful about what happened to him—or at least to relitigate it—but I never saw him blow up or lash out. In fact, he was always happy. He smiled a lot, and he had a general enthusiasm for being social. Heck, I remember numerous times I went to visit Connie during retirement, and each visit he made me feel like I had made his week: "Van! Oh my gosh, good to see you!" He'd drop whatever he was doing and give me his full attention. I always felt special.

A few years after we retired, Connie and I went to an old timers' game in Detroit. It was a bit gimmicky, but a good excuse to see all the pros again. They had a couple of skills challenges surrounding the game, and I agreed to participate in the shooting contest. The other old timers watched from the stands, including Connie.

The shooting contest placed you and your opponent on opposite ends of the floor. You had a set area from which you could shoot, and whomever made the most shots within the time limit won the round. The winner of each round advanced through the tournament bracket to the finals. Pretty simple.

Well, I was on that night, and I came out hot. *Bang. Bang. Bang.* I was making everything. Why had I retired again? *Bang. Bang. Bang.* I beat my first opponent easily, and the second, then I was on to the finals. I was feeling it.

The whistle blew to start the final round and I released my first shot. In. I took the next. In. My streak was alive and well. I found the rhythm of my shot and started counting my makes—six, seven, eight. At the same time, I tracked my opponent on the other side. He hit seven, then eight. It was going to be close.

I upped my pace. Eleven. Twelve.

My opponent didn't relent. Eleven. Twelve.

Thirteen for me.

Thirteen for him.

Fourteen for me.

He missed.

Time was running out. I had him. Fifteen. Sixteen. The buzzer. I clapped my hands and shook the other guys' hand. "Good game," I said. He smiled and said thanks. We stood next to one another and waited for the official count.

The announcer cleared his throat: "For Tom Van Arsdale: 16 shots!" A cheer from the crowd. I waved.

"And for his opponent: *17!*" I felt myself go stiff as the crowd cheered again. *What? I had him. I know I had him.* I watched the guy pass me and shake the scorekeeper's hand and collect the prize and I just stood there and tried to look gracious. In my head, I replayed the final over and over. *Had I miscounted?*

I showered off in the locker room afterward. I thought the water would give me some clarity, but nope, I came out figuratively and literally steaming. I was sure I had the count right. How could they have missed that? I didn't care about the prize, but I wanted the win. I was still a competitive old basketball player, after all! I couldn't catch a break.

After my shower I went back out to the floor to sit in the stands and watch the old timers' game. I looked up at the section reserved for the former players and I saw a space next to Connie Hawkins. I held my hand up. He saw me and waved me over.

"Hey Connie." I sat down and leaned back in the folding seat.

"Hey Tommy, good shooting out there."

"Thanks."

We were both quiet. On the court, the guys tipped off the first half.

After a moment, Connie said: "You know Tommy, you beat that guy."

I started a little and looked at him. "What?"

"You beat that guy in the shooting contest. I counted your shots."

I scoffed and shook my head. "Are you kidding me? That's what I thought! I was counting, too. I thought I had beaten him by one."

Connie nodded. "I had you by one point, too."

"Dang." I looked at the ground and sighed.

"What?" Connie asked.

"Should…should I have argued the call?" I looked up at him.

Connie seemed to think for a moment. He rested his elbows on his knees and his long fingers formed a little tent in front of his mouth. His eyebrows scrunched. Finally, he leaned back again. "No. You were right to let him have it."

"You think so?"

Connie looked me right in the eyes. He put on a warm smile. "Trust me, Tom. You did the right thing."

And I knew what he meant.

For some reason, that conversation with Connie made me feel better, even if he confirmed I had been wronged. He affirmed my convictions, and coming from him, that means a lot. Could there be a better judge of what's fair and not fair?

It's odd to me that Connie would sit up in the stands during that meaningless contest and count shots, but it fits his story to a tee: He had an eye for justice and what was right for people. Late in my career, not reaching my goals of making the playoffs and being on a winning team could have turned me into a desperate, selfish player, but people like Connie impress me for how they orient themselves toward other people when they have every reason to wallow in doom and gloom. It's possible to find contentment in basketball apart from records and championships. Connie was happy. I don't know how, but he empowered me to be happy, too.

***

"Ladies and gentlemen, tonight, before his final NBA game, please welcome three-time NBA All-Star and yourrrrrrr starting Phoenix Suns forward: Tom Van Arsdale!"

As I stepped onto the court, I just tried to look straight ahead. Kathy was on my left, and my mom was on my right. They each had one of my arms, but I think they were dragging me more than I was leading them. It's uneasy for me to be honored. It was April 10, 1977—the final game of my career. There was a small arrangement prepared for me at center court—flowers, a portrait, and an honorary trophy.

I felt a knot in my stomach as we reached the half court logo. When my mom and Kathy dropped my arms, I put my hands behind my back and looked at the floor. The eyes of the crowd made my neck prickle, and the PA announcer boomed in my ears. Some jittery kids came forward to present me with the portrait and flowers, and I did my best to smile and thank them and make them feel appreciated. But inside, I just wished we could start the game.

The PA announcer began articulating my accomplishments in the NBA, but I didn't pay too close attention. I remember hearing mention of my All-Star appearances and my scoring binges and some of the teams I had played for, but it was as if my responses were stopping just behind my face. I stayed stoic. At one point Kathy took my hand and squeezed it and I glanced at her and squeezed back. Was she responding to the words about me, or did she know I was uncomfortable? I was totally detached from the moment. I accepted the portrait (it's actually a beautiful composite of me in various basketball poses, with some artistic flourishes to show my speed; I ended up keeping it, and I've come to admire it quite a bit), but one of the kids with the flowers held back. Those weren't for me. What was going on?

"Tom isn't the only person we want to honor tonight. This other individual has been a fixture of the Suns organization for years now. She's one of our biggest fans, and certainly the biggest fan of her two sons. Ladies and gentlemen, a special round of applause for Hilda Van Arsdale!"

And my 67-year-old mom stepped forward to thundering applause. She was still wearing her big button-down coat after her flight from Indiana, and she adjusted her glasses and beamed at the presenters and took her flowers and did her best to say thank you over the cheers. Then she turned back to me, her arms full of roses, and came in for a hug.

Something bloomed in my throat and I leaned down and hugged my mom. She smelled like clover. I felt her stand a little taller in her shoes and she whispered in my ear. "I love you, Tom. You did it. You should be proud."

In my mind, I saw the dust from the Greenwood court swirling in the headlights of the parked cars. I smelled the plasticky leather of the Emmerich Manual bus seats. I felt the heat of the lights at Butler Fieldhouse, and heard the static of the car radio as I drove to law school. The Motown brass strutted through my memory, followed by Oscar snorting awake on the plane, and the smells of Kathy's dependable pre-game meals. I remembered Cousy's growl, and Connie's smile, and Dick's voice on the phone.

From my first game to now, my last, my mom had always been there. She set out her lawn chair and drove to Bloomington and stood silhouetted on the front porch and always, always waited at the other end of the phone. So, at my retirement ceremony, I held her tight.

"Be proud, Tommy," she said. She let go and gave me a nod and I wiped my eyes with an open hand. I tried taking deep breaths. The PA announcer closed the ceremony: "Ladies and gentlemen, one last time for Tom Van Arsdale!"

And this time, I looked up. The crowd rose to their feet, clapping, whistling, cheering. I closed my eyes for a moment, and I let it reach me. I smiled and went to wave, but it broke the seal on my feelings, and I felt myself start to lose it again. I laughed. I waved at the crowd. My friends. My family. My teammates. My peers. They clapped and clapped, and I met them there. My eyes went blurry and the colors mixed together. Purple and orange, like a sunset.

Chapter Twelve

Bobby Knight never had to look far to find something to be upset about, but on that particular day in Murmansk, Russia, with the harsh tundra wind swirling around us and the icy waters of the Kola bay prodding at our boots, he had a shorter fuse than usual.

"Where are all the goddamn fish?" he said.

There were 15 of us total—12 visitors and three Russian guides—on the Kola bay north of Murmansk. It was a few years after Dick and I retired, and Coach Knight had invited us and a few other friends on a fly-fishing trip he had scheduled and organized himself. It was an investment—we each paid $10,000 up front, and probably spent another $2,000 on cold-weather gear, camping equipment, and helicopter rides to the river—but it was worth it for the gorgeous scenery and the enticement of fishing the legendary Russian salmon run. The only problem was, so far, none of us had felt even a nibble. Knight's casts out into the water were becoming more and more pointed.

"Fuckin' fish," he muttered. "Where's their motivation? They have a perfectly good goddamn lure right there, and they won't jump." He twitched his rod.

The water was still.

Despite the lackadaisical fish, it had been a typically fantastic trip with Coach Knight. Dick and I traveled with him often after the two of us retired, because Coach Knight knew how to leverage his celebrity on a trip (even if he didn't love

211

being a celebrity). At the height of his championship-level success at Indiana, Knight could put his foot in just about any door. On this particular trip to Russia, we enjoyed a behind-the-scenes tour of the State Hermitage Museum in St. Petersburg, and we met the coaches for the Russian Olympic basketball team before heading up to Murmansk for our private fishing adventure. Knight had international appeal. Maybe not everyone liked him in those days, but given the chance, everyone was eager to associate with him.

Knight knew Dick before the rest of our family. The two of them had connected in the late 1960s, when Knight was still coaching at Army and Dick was training with the Knicks at West Point. After Indiana hired Knight in 1971, Knight reached out to Dick for intel. He asked him about being a Hoosier, what Indiana was like, what Dick enjoyed and didn't enjoy about the school—anything that would give him a sense of the local flavor. And while Dick was thorough, Coach Knight is dogged and committed. He asked Dick who else he could speak with, and Dick said Knight could talk to our mom, Hilda.

So, Coach Knight called her. And of course, they hit it off.

Mom was always a massive Hoosiers fan, but after Dad passed away, Indiana became one of her lifelines. She'd drive down to Bloomington for every home game, sit in the stands, and cheer her heart out. She brought friends along (at least, the friends who would actually watch the game instead of trying to chat with her—if Mom accidentally invited someone who just wanted to yap, it would end up being their only invite) and garnered a little visibility and eventually became close with everyone from the athletic director to the team doctors. She had a little community within the program, so when Coach Knight came aboard, she naturally looked to adopt him into her extended family.

Coach Knight and Mom became so close that sometimes, when Coach Knight wanted to escape Bloomington and be somewhere a little more relaxed for a weekend, he'd stay at Mom's house, sleeping just a few yards away from our old dirt court. In return for Mom's hospitality, Knight would give her premium tickets so she could sit closer than usual at the next game. Mom just loved that. The only thing that might spoil those games was if Coach Knight lost his composure and made a scene. Mom didn't mind the demonstration, but she worried Coach Knight would find himself in trouble. It really was like he was her third son.

Coach Knight and my sweet old mom were an odd pairing, but they fit. She didn't mind his language and color—Mom had a farmgirl upbringing, so she was used to rowdiness and surliness—and he admired her perseverance and grit. Plus, Mom knew basketball really well, and since that was and still is what Coach Knight likes to talk about most, it thrilled him. Their relationship eventually trickled down to Dick and me.

***

The salmon trips notwithstanding, I realized how close Dick and I had become with Coach Knight in the summer of 1984, when Knight invited Dick and me back to Indiana to play a scrimmage with the 1984 Olympic team he was coaching (this team would eventually win the gold medal at the Los Angeles games). This was before pros could be in the Olympics, but the team was loaded with amateur stars: Patrick Ewing, Steve Alford, Sam Perkins, and Chris Mullin included.

Dick and I showed up and immediately felt out of place. We were the oldest guys there by a mile—42, both of us. Even the non-Olympians on our scrimmage team were younger, sharper, and just plain better players than we were at that point, and I was afraid we'd be embarrassed. But Coach Knight kept us on the bench, out of the line of fire, except for a couple minutes apiece in the second half. It was a gesture of respect, sort of like when a pro team lets their deep bench guys play for a few minutes during the last game of a season. A thank-you for being here, in basketball language.

Well, I checked in and was immediately assigned to a young player expected to go very high in that year's NBA draft—his name was Michael Jordan. It was like guarding a buzzsaw. Michael cooked me like a backyard hamburger, and Coach Knight subbed me out before I took too much damage. Not my best performance, but it didn't matter. That was a meaningful invitation from Knight, an honor, really. Dick and I were included in an Olympic Games.

If only the salmon knew we were so significant.

Coach Knight sighed through his nose like a bull and twitched his lure a few more times. The fly leapt off the water. He was losing his finesse. "Damn it," Knight said. He reached back and cast again. The air was tense. I wondered if Pompei felt like this before Vesuvius exploded.

One of the Russian guides was watching Knight, and after this little show, he turned to me. He was an engineer from St. Petersburg—the Russian economy was so bad at the time that lots of Russian engineers, doctors, and lawyers had to find work outside their field—and he had hard lines in his face and a black beard. "Why did you come up this time of the year?" he asked.

I frowned. "What do you mean? We came up here to catch the salmon."

The guide frowned. "But the salmon run is over. There are no salmon here."

I almost fumbled my fishing pole. "What?"

Dick was next to me. He overheard. "What? There aren't any salmon at all? Are you kidding me?"

The other guys up and down the shoreline caught our tone and saw our faces. *What was that, fellas?* Coach Knight looked up from his line. Uh oh.

The guide turned toward the group, unaware his next words would be the equivalent of slapping a hibernating bear across the cheek. "The salmon run has been over for weeks. There are no salmon in the bay. We thought you knew this."

Coach Knight's whole body seemed to ripple. I once watched a nature documentary about a color-changing seahorse, and when this creature was agitated, it would begin flashing reds, blues, and greens in a strobe-like effect. I had never seen anything like it until I saw the dazzling array of colors emerge in Coach Knight's countenance at that moment. He looked like he was about to puke he was so angry. If I printed what he said next, I'd go to hell, so I'll censor him for this section:

Coach Knight turned to the guide. "[I'm sorry, sir. Could you repeat yourself, please?"]

The guide: "The salmon run is over. They have gone from this water."

Knight: "[Oh, dear. Well that's a real pain in the patooty. What shall we do now?]"

"I would advise you go somewhere else. The fishing will be very difficult for you here."

"[Well butter my biscuits and ring the dinner bell, this is a disappointment. Let's retire to the hotel for a meal and some refreshment.]"

"Should I call the helicopter?"

"[We'd all appreciate that so much. The sooner the better, but no rush.]"

"OK." The guide raised his radio. "We are ready to be picked up. And the coach says if you do not hurry, he will put his boot in your asshole."

As we waited for the chopper, Coach Knight cussed out the river, the cold, the $10,000 cost, the salmon, and then me, for "standing around like a jackass and scratching my crotch while the fish swam away." We all just laughed. This was classic Bobby Knight. You didn't take it personally. He just needed to let it all out.

But when we arrived back at the cabins, there was a holdup at the front door and we all had to stand in a line to go inside. Coach Knight was in front of me. I looked down and saw that his pants had sagged a little and the top of his striped Hanes boxer shorts were poking above his waistband. I grinned to myself. "You know, Bob," I said. "You better be careful.

When the leader of the group steers everybody wrong, his buddies might lose a little respect for him."

Coach Knight grumbled. "What are you talking about, Tommy?"

And I grabbed his boxer shorts and hoisted them as high as I could. "You can't let a bunch of old players get the best of you!" I shouted.

Coach Knight yelped like a wounded rhinoceros, clapped his hands over his butt, and whirled around. His eyes narrowed into search-and-destroy mode and his fists clenched. I jumped back into the other guys, my goofy smile frozen on my face, and behind me all our buddies were laughing and hooting and teasing Bob. Coach Knight stepped forward—I could've sworn he was about to clock me—but then he saw all of our humor and lowered his hands. A small smile threatened to tug at his mouth. He waved us off. "This is why I never take a trip with young people."

Just a few minutes later, Coach Knight cooled off, and for the rest of the week, we all had a nice time hanging at the cabins. It wasn't a $10,000 hotel, but the memories have to be worth something.

***

The least that could be said about Coach Knight's infamous temper is that he doesn't mind saying what he thinks. As his friend, it was a great source of humor, but I know for many, his tirades were hurtful. When Coach Knight was young, his tantrums were perceived as passionate, but as he grew older, they took on a negative undertone. He was out of coaching by the mid-2000s, and while his numerous records did a lot to solidify his legacy as a tactician and strategist, his personal legacy in basketball was tarnished and dark. As his health declined, he retreated further and further from the public eye.

Coach Knight and I spoke often during that period. He was really affected by the way basketball ostracized him. Bob is a delicate combination of loyalty and sensitivity, so he internalizes rejection at a deep, personal level. As a whole, I actually think Coach Knight is hurt very easily. That's why he's so transparent with his feelings. He wants you to take him or leave him. Then he knows where you stand. Then he won't feel betrayed. Obviously, there's a duality to his transparency, some good and some bad, but as his friend, I wish some of Coach Knight's goodness was more well-known, because he's very discrete about it. Coach Knight has always been very quick, even eager, to help me when I ask for it. He wants his friends to succeed, and he's happy to use his influence to facilitate that. He's drawn to humility and hard work, and he rewards those who exemplify those things. He doesn't suffer know-it-alls, and he hates cockiness—he just wants people to be as real as he is. Honestly, I think he's brilliant. And I think he's intense. And serious. Above all, across the heroic and villainous stages of his life, he's been one of my closest, most persistent friends.

Bob has become more mellow now. One time, we were wrapping up a conversation (about basketball—it's still all he wants to talk about) when he said, "Alright Tom. Take care of yourself. I love you."

I almost dropped the phone.

The old Coach Knight is still there. He likes telling off-color jokes and he's never stopped cussing, but I see Bob more now. He's kind, and lovable, and he's careful to tell people how much they've meant to him over the years. I think Bob's age is catching up to him a bit and he's thinking about his life in a more wistful way. We talk about God sometimes, and it seems little by little, we're venturing beyond basketball to discuss the relationships we made in the sport and the other things most important to us. Bob really loves people. What's more, I think he likes people, too.

And as Bob has approached the twilight of his life, the basketball world has come back to him. He's rekindled a lot of old friendships and has reconnected with plenty of his peers and former players. I think that's the final special thing I have to say about basketball. Generally, our culture today doesn't allow for second chances, but basketball gave one to someone as controversial and polarizing and abrasive as Coach Knight. That's really unique. There's grace in the basketball community. Once you enter into our family, you're in our family for life.

**

Before writing this book, I saw my NBA career from the perspective of someone who was a member of an out-group. I didn't make the playoffs. I didn't win a championship. I didn't play for a winning team. That lens—being an unlucky have-not among so many haves—worked its way under my skin over the years, and I actually pitched this book as an airing of my grievances. I was ready to vent about the unfairness I felt, the bias with which we view NBA legacies, and how sports culture panders to modern players who enjoy extended schedules and load management and charter planes and nutritional and medicinal science. I was mad.

But after spending over a year with this book, thinking about all the highs and lows of my career, I learned to broaden my perspective and raise my eyes above my disappointments. There were no haves and have-nots in basketball. Not really. The truth is, we were all lucky to be in the NBA. It's a spoiled experience. People took care of us and admired us and all we had to do was show up to practice and play a game we love. I didn't recognize how easy I had it. Maybe a lot of guys missed that, too. Of course, I do think some guys are more gifted than others, and some are luckier than others, but Bill Russell, Oscar Robertson, Jerry West and Tom Van Arsdale all had the same NBA privileges. That's special.

I think about Bob Knight as I close this book because writing this book took me on a similar journey as my friend. I used to be angry and bitter toward basketball, but this process brought all the blessings of my life in sports to the fore, and I gained a new appreciation for the community and belonging I found in the NBA. Today, even at 77 years old, I can call anybody from my era and share a connection over what we achieved and how hard we worked. I couldn't have anything more valuable than that kinship this side of heaven. It's where I find my happiness.

Some of the most cherished moments of my retired life come when I have some downtime at the art studio I share with Dick in downtown Scottsdale. If things are quiet around sunset, I take a chair outside to feel the nighttime breeze and watch the traffic cruise down Main street. As the palm trees turn to indigo silhouettes and the light fades, I pull out my phone and scroll through my contacts, looking at all the players I keep in touch with. Then, I just pick a name, and I call. A quick tap and I put the phone against my ear.

Click "Van! How you doing? How's it going?"

It's the fastest way to make me smile. We talk until the sun goes down, sharing stories, asking about families, remembering things.

Over the course of writing this book, I called Oscar Robertson, Bob Cousy, Tom Chambers, Dave Cowens, Alvan Adams, Jerry Sichting, Sam Jones, Dave Bing, Bill Walton, Babe Pryor, Keith Erickson, Fred Carter, Steve Mix, Jon McGlocklin, Al Harden, Tom Bolyard, and Steve Redenbaugh. Every conversation was an affirmation, each of them enthusiastic, excited, as if no time had passed: "Tom! I'm so glad you called. How's Phoenix?"

My friends and I are growing older now. It's been 50 years since we played. But talking on the phone feels like time traveling. We go back, we compete, we tease one another and laugh—it feels good to think about being young and strong again. Our generation is often accused of "reliving the glory days," like we should leave the past behind, but I have found nothing to be more essential in my old age than running down memory lane with my friends. Our conversations rekindle the best times of my life, moments I can't take for granted anymore, moments that might disappear eventually. Talking about the past makes us aware of all the change we've experienced, and how that has shaped the ideas we care about and the opportunities we have to communicate those ideas to people who can carry them forward. My friends are inspiring to me; I admire them. Being in their family changed my life, and it's wonderful to celebrate that together.

***

Along Highway 431 in Indianapolis, there is a mural called 'The Runners.' It depictes multiple generations of Hoosiers—people of all ages, races, backgrounds, occupations, and degrees of fame—running together in a large, unified crowd. Kurt Vonnegut is there, and so is the Black cyclist Major Taylor, the actress Anne Baxter, and coach john Wooden, among others. Dick and I are up there, too.

The NBA can pull you in so many different directions, so fast and without warning, that it becomes easy to miss things. You never have a chance to step back and see the whole picture, and the great benefit of my retirement has been seeing my career for what it was. There was no climactic moment of triumph or storybook ending, but I was a part of a beautiful history. That's my success. Peace doesn't come when everything goes right. Peace comes when you're right with how everything goes.

I say goodbye to my friends, hang up the phone, and sit still for a moment in front of the art studio. Around me, the streetlights flicker on, the desert critters scurry to their homes, and the young people chat and laugh on their way to dinner downtown. It's nice being still. Things aren't perfect, but they're the way they're supposed to be. It's been a long journey for me, but now I'm home.

The End

ACKNOWLEDGEMENTS

A special thanks to my brother Dick, Bob Hammel, Michael Daswick, Richard Murian, Ken Wells, Freddie Carter, Tom Chambers, Steve Mix, Jon McGlocklin, Jerry Sichting, and especially my wife Kathy, who encouraged me to finish this book and led the effort to get it published.

The net proceeds from the sale of JOURNEY MAN will be donated to RETT Syndrome research in honor of our granddaughter

MINNA CATHERINE VAN ARSDALE

ABOUT THE AUTHORS

Tom Van Arsdale was born in the great state of Indiana, the heartbeat of the game of basketball. Alongside his twin brother he became Co-Mr Basketball in the state, at Indianapolis Manual High School. Tom was named All American at Indiana University, and spent 12 years in the NBA, becoming a three time NBA All Star. At the age of 77, Tom wrote this book detailing his reflections of his time in the NBA.

Learn more about Tom's endeavors at www.vanarsdaleart.com and www.jacquesclothesline.com

Tyler Daswick is a graduate of the Medill School of Journalism at Northwestern University. He's a writer and editor for Hearst Magazines. His work has appeared in *ESPN, Grantland, The Chicago Reader, Men's Health, Popular Mechanics,* and *Runner's World.* He also writes the newsletter DudeNotes, Notes About Faith for Dudes, which circulates weekly to dudes (and non-dudes). He lives in Bethlehem, Pennsylvania.

tylerdaswick@gmail.com

Made in the USA
Middletown, DE
19 July 2022